"I wish Tom lived next door. I'd want to "run home from work" most every day to sit on the front porch with him and hear his deep, soft voice paint vivid word pictures of a unique life, well lived in the presence and pursuit of our loving Heavenly Father. We don't live next door to each other. I do, however, have this book--the next best way for me to be inspired by Tom's words to fall in love with Jesus anew and more deeply each morning, seeking to live life more selflessly, expectantly, and more attuned to God, Himself. Thanks, Tom, for being a faithful follower of He who loves us best and always. Thanks for writing this book--it is a blessing. I am privileged to call you friend."

Mark Haskins
Professor, University of Virginia

"One of the greatest gifts in life is a sage. Someone who has gone before us and can communicate honestly their success and failures. You'll know when you meet this kind of person because you will fall in love with them. Tom and Barb show us a Kingdom where the very worst things in life can turn out to be the very best things in life. So you have been warned, if you read this book be prepared to fall in love again."

Jeff and Dana Andrechyn
Expeditions of the Heart

Tom and Barbara Mohn have been trusted friends and mentors for over 25 years. Tom's stories of walking with Martin Luther King, radio hosting for Oral Roberts, experiencing both great success and setbacks in life and ministry and many others will draw you in, revealing the hand of a loving, faithful God. His insights found in the last section will help you keep your own walk in perspective. How do I know? Because that's what they do for me. Enjoy!!

Lance Thollander
President, Hope Builders International;
Author: Walking the Galatian Road, Moving from Law to Life

Published by Mohn Ministries, Inc.
www.mohnministriesbookstore.com

Edited by Lance Thollander
Cover illustration by Steve Rhom
E-Book by Pixel Dust, LLC

ISBN 978-0-578-13717-9

E-Book available at:
WWW.MOHNMINISTRIESBOOKSTORE.COM

GOOD MORNING, BROTHER PILGRIM...

ONE MAN'S JOURNEY IN FOLLOWING GOD

BY TOM MOHN

FOREWORD

You hold in your hands a treasure, though you may not know that if you don't know Tom Mohn. As a writer, I know it is all but impossible to get someone to read a memoir written by a person they don't know. That's why celebrities can get away with it, but real people rarely do.

So before you are tempted to put this book down let me introduce you to Tom, a man who over the last ten years has become a trusted and valued friend. I've lived in his home, watched how he relates to his wife and children, and have had many rich conversations about the life of Jesus with him. He is deeply loved and appreciated by friends and family, which says a lot. He's lived his life with wit and humor that disarms people with joy and blesses them with his wisdom.

I can easily say that Tom is one of the most genuine and authentic men I've ever known. And that's no small compliment. I've met many who talk about God but whose lives in no way reflect the truths they pretend to espouse. One honestly admitted to me that he wasn't even trying to live the things he wrote about, but was simply marketing a book to the Christian audience. This book is an honest reflection of a life well lived from someone who has over the course of decades learned how to walk with God through the triumphs and tragedies of life. Through it all a passionate and tender grace is shaped in him that exudes from his life to help others discover how they, too, can live in a growing fullness of God's love.

Gently, through each season of his life, God keeps inviting Tom into a deeper journey, away from the artificiality of manmade religion and into a transforming relationship with an ever-present God. This is quite a journey from husband and father to reluctant pastor, civil rights supporter, radio personality, and Bible teacher. One man called him the "Forrest Gump of Christianity" as his life intersects with the likes of Martin Luther King, Jr., Oral Roberts, Derek Prince, and Gene Edwards.

You will be enriched by the humorous and honest stories he tells and the lessons he has learned along the way. Some are stunningly supernatural, while others rise out very normal experiences. He's refreshingly honest with his mistakes and failures and the persistent unanswered questions that have risen out of his journey. In the end it is a story of transformation and grace and how learning to follow Jesus is a bit of trial and error as you navigate whatever comes your way with an ear cocked in his direction. Miles down the journey you'll sense Tom's contentment in God's unfolding work and hopefully hunger for it as well.

And after you've finished his story, stay tuned for the appendix, where you'll find even more treasure in the articles Tom has written about the most important life lessons that influenced his journey. They alone are worth whatever you might pay for this book. I enjoy Tom as a friend and older brother in the faith. If you already know him, you won't need this forward. If you don't know him yet, this book is a great place to start.

Wayne Jacobsen

Author, *He Loves Me: Learning to Live in the Father's Affection*

ACKNOWLEDGEMENTS

First let me thank all those at Hope Builders International who encouraged me to write this book. That is Mark and Leslie, Jeff and Dana, Ricky and Donna, Lance and Christie. A further word must be written thanking Lance for his expertise as an editor and his patience in working with me in this my first writing endeavor. There are no words that can honor enough the love of my life and Kingdom partner of 52+ years, Barbara. Her steadfastness and love for Jesus has supplied our family with wisdom that many times brought clarity, healing and release in our continuing adventure.

There are so many lives that over the decades have blessed, healed, taught, disciplined and still continue to encourage us into Jesus and His Kingdom. I know I will miss some but here are a few: Edna Hutchins a retired Methodist missionary, E. Stanley Jones who was introduced to us by Edna, Rev Tommy Tyson, the first chaplain at Oral Roberts University, Dr. Frost, a professor at ORU, Rev Charlie Groves, Dr. Chuck Farah, Rev Bill Sanders, and lastly, the great numbers of those who walked with us through Bread of Life Fellowship and school.

We have been encouraged onward in our journey by the lives of our faithful children, who continue to press on in the Lord Jesus: Rebecca and her husband Bryan, Paul and his wife DeVon, Thomas and his wife Beth, Matthew and his wife Andrea, and Sarah and her husband Steve. These along with our 21 grand-children continue to press us into the Lord.

Finally, I give all honor to my life giving Savior, Jesus Christ, the proclaimer and continuing Lord of God's Kingdom.

DEDICATION

John 5:39-40

"You have your heads in your Bibles constantly because you think you'll find eternal life there. But you miss the forest for the trees. These Scriptures are all about me! And here I am, standing right before you, and you aren't willing to receive from me the life you say you want." ~The Message

"I dedicate this book to the thousands of people I have met in my 50+ years of following Jesus, who have seriously struggled to find Him but who sadly were led only to the Bible for truth and that in a legalistic way. A way, whether intended or not, replaced Jesus with the Bible. These words in John remind me over and over again that true life is found only in Jesus Himself. If you find yourself in the above category, I hope as you read my story, you too, will be brought into the wonder that is found in simply knowing Jesus. As you do, the Scriptures themselves will become a friend beyond words, constantly lifting up and magnifying Jesus."

~ Tom

CONTENTS

Good Morning, Brother Pilgrim

PREFACE

Like all who have come to know Jesus as Lord of our lives, my wife, Barbara, and I were known by Him long before we recognized Him. We were trying to find our way in the dark and descending more deeply into despair. I as a Methodist pastor was preaching from Psychology Today; and Barb was planning her escape from the mundane to the glamorous.

Our moments of birth into the Kingdom happened within a week of each other in the early spring of 1965. Like all new believers we discovered a wonderful gift—the ability to hear the voice of our Shepherd, Jesus Christ. We rediscovered the Scriptures with new passion with the Spirit of Jesus helping us see fresh new truth. We and our growing family were launched on the adventure that has captured us ever since—exploring the Kingdom of God with its glorious and eccentric citizens and occupations—both elegant and simple. On the following pages you will read the stories of how the Lord was at work in my life as a child, in our lives as young adults, and then on into full adulthood. These incidences reveal God's care for each one of us before we even know who He is, an amazing truth that will find resonance in your own heart and life.

We recently retired as pastors of the church we founded in 1970—Bread of Life Fellowship in Tulsa OK. While I, Tom, was dealing with the joys & heartaches of pastoral ministry, Barb was being mentored in a more hidden school—the one whose curriculum included caring for and loving five children, several young adults, and aging, infirm, in-laws. During the past 45 years or so, both of us have learned (through inadequacy & desperation) to access the presence and power of the Lord Jesus and His love.

Now that our five children are married with children of their own (21 all together), we look forward with excitement to the next leg in our Kingdom adventure. Barb has been deeply involved in teaching and counseling troubled women at a homeless shelter in our community, and she has been involved in foreign missions to Cuba, India, Mexico, and Russia. Several years ago, she joined me in teaching a Bible study which I had taught alone for 20 years. In addition, we have held week-end teaching seminars at various churches in the U.S., the U.K., and Norway.

Barb finished her college degree and I have been sharing Kingdom life with small groups of believers, young and old, meeting together in homes. Some of the people we have mentored are scattered throughout the world—broadcasting Kingdom seed wherever they are sent.

We are eternally grateful for the many of God's people who have touched our lives either personally or through books. One woman in particular must be highlighted: Edna Hutchins was a retired Methodist missionary who spent 50 or more years in India. Edna's life was so contagious that at a time when we were in darkness, we knew she had something more than empty religion. She introduced us to the real, personal, Jesus. She later would introduce us to books of E. Stanley Jones and his light concerning the real gospel of The Kingdom of God. These and many others were our spiritual mentors.

For over 50 years, we have been exploring and discovering the varied landscapes of the Lord's eternal Kingdom. It is infinite and ever growing. We are debtors to all those Kingdom citizens who have gone before us, but most of all to the initiator of it all, our Father God and His Son, Jesus, who made our citizenship possible.

Chapter 1

FROM SELMA TO SALVATION

Marching with Dr. King

I COULDN'T BELIEVE what I was seeing on the TV news. Could local law enforcement really do such a thing? Could Jim Clark, the sheriff, really mean outside agitators caused this? Was Martin Luther King Jr. a communist conspirator? These questions rolled over and over in my mind. Then I witnessed the dogs being unleashed on men, women, and children in the streets of Birmingham and Selma, Alabama.

Could I, Tom Mohn, youth pastor at a Methodist Church, just idly sit and watch this happen? Up to this time, my idea of Christian ministry was a response to vocational guidance tests. The tests indicated I would find fulfillment in the social services, psychology, or law—the helping professions. My being in the ministry certainly was not the result of a call of God or a religious experience of any kind. My faith was in political and social activism. I believed with the right people in public office and the right legislation we could change society. My background was conservative, and I was amazed that many of my co-workers and fellow students had difficulty reconciling conservative values with any kind of social conscience. As far as I was concerned, social activism was the gospel.

In retrospect, I realize God was setting me up for a life-altering change of direction. While the civil rights battle lines were forming, other more subtle influences were challenging my spirit. An article in Collier's Magazine told of a newly discovered spiritual phenomenon—glossalalia (speaking in tongues); a retired missionary to India named Edna Hutchins loved us with fearless compassion and generosity; and a book called The Cross and the Switchblade introduced us to a God of life-changing power. Finally, my genuine relationships with my fellow employees, most of whom were black, were used by God to prepare me for Selma and its aftermath.

One more converging element involved the municipal government. The city of Evanston had a petition on open housing which was being discussed and, hopefully, would be put on a ballot. Its purpose was to prosecute any realtor who didn't show all available properties to everyone, regardless of race. It was hotly contested in this very conservative city. I was very much for it and found it difficult to understand why anyone would oppose it. The stage had already been set by an invisible director when I viewed that news broadcast.

"How could one human being do that to another?" My theology did not make room for such cruelty—not if mankind was born intrinsically good. This same theology ridiculed the reality of evil and the fall of man, essentially eliminating any need for a personal Savior. I believed society could save itself with righteous laws and equal opportunities.

Following the brutality in Selma, Martin Luther King put out a call for clergy from all over the United States to join him in Selma and walk together to Birmingham in a demonstration of solidarity and protest. The next morning found me on a plane from Chicago to Atlanta where I would then fly to Birmingham. On the flight from Chicago, I discovered more than twenty clergymen from the Chicago area on board. They also had responded to Martin Luther King's plea for support. I was drawn to a quiet, little Jewish rabbi. I asked why, at his advanced age, he was on board the flight. His response was quiet and penetrating.

After a short pause, he said, "Perhaps if Christian priests and Jewish rabbis had marched with us in the late 30's, Hitler could have been stopped." He continued by saying that following the war he had taken a vow to stand up for the persecuted. "I will not forget, and I will not be silent," he said.

The conversation with this rabbi moved me deeply as I talked with him nearly all the way to Atlanta. Arriving in Atlanta, I joined the hundreds of clergy that were heading toward Selma. One incident at the airport was a harbinger of the storm into which we were heading. I sat down at a lunch counter to grab a bite to eat.

The surly waiter, visibly troubled by our presence in the South, cursed under his breath, "Why the hell are damned, northern agitators comin' down to cause trouble. We were getting along jest fine until that rabble rousin' King started stirrin' up trouble."

I was taken aback by his anger and was mulling over a response when a Roman Catholic priest sat down beside me. His collar elicited even more disgust from the waiter than I had received. The waiter evidently was convinced that all Catholics (especially priests) were secret agents of the Pope. The priest was the recipient of yet another barrage of insults. He then responded in a strong Irish brogue, "Ah, Praise the Saints! This will be a good time to fast!" Turning to me, he asked if I would like to join him in a fast. Awkwardly, I said, "Sure," almost meaning it.

It was late in the afternoon when we arrived in Selma. I was surprised at the number of people already there. We drove to the black section of town and partook of some wonderful barbeque, served on wax paper. The little place was packed with laughing people from all over the country. Each one of us was asked to tell our story of why we had responded to Martin

Luther King's call for clergy. With slight variations, most of us had similar stories. Our little group of six who had ridden together from Birmingham decided to hang out together. We had already become fast friends—knit together by a common purpose.

While we were discussing where to spend the night, a young black woman overheard us. She sweetly interrupted us and said her mother would like us to come to their apartment for the night. She said we'd have to sleep on the floor or couches, but that we would be comfortable. We quickly agreed.

We drove over to a housing project and, as we unloaded, noticed many people coming out to greet us. Dozens of other visitors were also being welcomed into apartments. An older woman, perhaps in her seventies, greeted us. She could have been from "Hollywood central casting." She reminded me of every older black woman I had seen in the movies. She was plump, joyful, inviting, with a graciousness that was disarming. You immediately felt as though you were in the presence of great suffering and dignity. She busily went about making us as comfortable as possible. I ended up on the floor with a heavy, soft quilt and a glossy, red, satin pillow with something biblical embroidered on it.

After we were settled in, the six of us gathered in the downstairs living room to join our host family and a few of their friends. We were asked why we had come, so each of us shared our stories. After an hour and a half we felt like old friends. It was about 11:00 P.M. when we all realized just how tired we were. We were about to break up when our hostess said she wanted to share something with us.

A kind of quiet, powerful, awe swept through the room as though some hidden command had been given. She had our attention. She told us she was the firstborn of slaves. Her parents had been slaves as had her grandparents. Her parents had stayed in the South following emancipation. She remembered hearing how her grandparents had "jumped the broom" to begin their marriage. She talked of her Daddy and Momma with great pride and love.

As she was ending her moving story, she recounted the unforgettable hope her mother had planted in her—a hope she had passed on to her own children. Her mother said that God would one day deliver them just as "Ole Mose" had delivered the Hebrew children. In a voice trembling with emotion, our hostess said, "Thank you, Jesus. I am seeing the beginning of the end to bondage!" At this, she began to cry and came to each of us and hugged us with one of those unforgettable hugs. We were humbled by her gratitude and wept with her. After we prayed together, we said our "goodnights" and went to bed.

My head had hardly hit the little satin pillow when it was morning. The smell of biscuits and gravy filled the house. Somehow, we all finished our bathroom needs with only one bathroom then sat down to breakfast at 7:30.

We were to meet at the African Methodist Episcopal church around 9 o'clock so the Student Nonviolent Coordinating Committee (SNCC) volunteers could give us some tips on the march and how to protect ourselves. Dr. King was due to arrive sometime before noon.

After thanking our host family, we all loaded into the van and headed for downtown Selma. Thousands of people had gathered and the atmosphere was electric. The SNCC volunteers began to show us how to protect ourselves from clubs, cattle prods, dogs, and rocks, but most importantly from the epithets. We were not to respond but to bear silently any words or blows. If there were children in the march, we were to try our best to keep ourselves between them and any harm. We were instructed to march four abreast, with the children in the middle.

We had just finished this briefing when Dr. King arrived. He spoke to us all from the steps of the church. He thanked us for responding so quickly and being willing to follow his principles of non-violence. He was interrupted by loud, strident questions from detractors in the crowd. "Dr. King, are you aware there are Communist sympathizers in this gathering? What are you going to do about it?" Without raising his voice, he evenly acknowledged the possibility but added, "This is a religious movement based on the Judeo-Christian scriptures, historical testimony, and man's search for freedom from tyranny of all kinds—including communism."

Beginning in a downtown square of Selma, the lines formed. For the first time, I became aware of another large crowd which had also gathered. This one was enraged, vocal, and restless. The angry crowd lined the street we were to pass. The marchers slowly began walking hand-in-hand, four-a-breast, with the children in the middle. The young black boy to my right held my hand tightly as he pleaded wide-eyed, "You ain't gonna leave me, is you, Suh?" His grip relaxed a little as I smiled down at him and assured him I would not.

I briefly looked up at the overcast sky to explain the wet drops I felt on my face and neck. The drops were not falling from the sky. They were being spewed from the cursing mouths of the men, women, and children who lined the street. The enraged crowd was being held at bay by the reluctant police and their dogs. The anger of the mob served to deepen our commitment to the demonstration of peaceful solidarity—Black, White, Jew and Gentile, young and old—walked on together.

The ancient ethnic hatred of generations came into focus in one young mother's face. Straining to hurl vile racial epithets, her countenance was twisted into an ugly caricature as she poured out her poisonous anger upon us. The baby in her arms stared wide-eyed, and her toddler son joined in the taunts, faithfully imitating his mother.

The "Law" was there, some with dogs on chains. The police

would let the dogs charge at us and then pull them back at the last minute, producing great laughter from the angry crowd. Slowly, our four abreast line began to move. As it did, I pulled the little boy on the inside closer to protect him from thrown rocks and debris.

I was terrified. I had never experienced so much hate in my life. Between the jeering crowds, the dogs, and the stones, I realized that someone might easily be killed. I remember praying underneath my breath for courage and to not respond in anger.

As the line moved, someone began to sing *Amazing Grace*. One-by-one, the marchers joined in. As we sang, courage began to flow through this long line of marchers until we were caught up in an overwhelming unity. When we began singing *We Shall Overcome* my heart swelled with deep joy and pride. I was surprised by the total absence of fear and the deep hope in my heart. I would have gladly given my life for this cause.

Together we marched several blocks when the line stopped. Police were blocking the road ahead. Martin Luther King and other leaders from the Southern Christian Leadership Conference were talking with the officers. Red lights were flashing all over the place as we strained to pick up on the conversation. Finally, those ahead began to pass back what was being discussed. They were saying we had no permission to march on state highways or county roads. The officers could not insure our protection. We were stopped at the bridge because we did not have the appropriate permits. If we continued, we agitators would be immediately jailed. Dr. King and the other leaders of the march agreed to continue the march in the morning. He thanked us all for coming and asked us to return to wherever we were staying. He recognized that some might have to return to their homes, but many more clergy were still arriving from all over the United States.

Just before Dr. King dismissed the crowd of marchers, he

and the others dropped to their knees and began to pray. The entire line, from front to rear, melted into an orderly wave as spontaneous prayer and praise broke out. Praise swept from front to rear and back again. There was laughing, crying, singing, hugging and, most curious of all, a total unawareness of the angry crowd with its spitting, rock throwing, dogs, and cursing. Timelessness enveloped us. Then it stopped, as spontaneously as it had started, and we all began to rejoin our respective little groups. We dispersed homeward guided by an unseen hand.

Suddenly, I became aware that I was sore all over my body and wet from head to foot with spit. I remember pulling my overcoat collar up to better protect myself. I looked at the little boy who was still holding my hand tightly. His grin is still indelibly etched on my mind, even these many decades later.

Chapter 2

THE AFTERMATH

Soon the six of us were together again, loaded into the van, and headed back to the house where we had spent the night. As we arrived, the ladies we had met the night before were also back, asking if we were hungry. We had decided on route that we would like to repay their kindnesses by buying lunch for all. The dear sisters protested but we prevailed, and two from our group went to the store, purchasing enough food to feed an army. After they had returned, the six of us began to prepare the food, hamburgers, hot dogs, BBQ, potato salad, coleslaw, soft drinks, chips and dips. Soon we were eating, laughing, and telling our stories of the morning march. All of us experienced the same things, especially the racial slurs, cursing, spitting, threatening and rocks, stones and attack dogs. Everyone one of us was still in awe about the spiritual wave that flowed up and down the long line. We also thought it odd that we had regrouped so easily.

After the late lunch and cleanup, we talked about what we should do that night and the following day. Our group consisted of a black Episcopal priest who drove the van, a Lutheran pastor, a Catholic priest, another Baptist preacher, a rabbi and me. After talking with our hosts and praying, the unanimous decision was that we should each return home, making space for the many that were arriving. We all felt good about this and spent the next couple of hours talking and sharing. Soon the sun was down and we realized we had better pack up and head for the airport to get our flight to Atlanta. As we parted amidst hugs and tears, we also expressed gratitude that, aside from some sore places from stones and the spitting, no one had been seriously injured. We thanked God and the media for protection.

As we piled into the VW van, waved our goodbyes, and headed out of the neighborhood, our driver pointed out that it had now been several hours since we had eaten and that food was difficult to get at the airports. He suggested we pick up a bite at a place he knew of before we left. We arrived at the BBQ place where we had first eaten when we arrived. It was packed with many of us who were leaving and many new people who had come. We waited a few minutes for a table and once again enjoyed some of the finest BBQ I had ever eaten. I'm sure the owner had never done this much business in his life. I'm equally sure he and the waitresses had never received better tips. Everyone just wanted to bless them. Laughter and joy filled the place until our driver said we had to go or we would miss our flight. He left to get the van and bring it around to the front. Again, we said goodbye to our new friends and walked out front beneath a brightly burning street light.

Another man was standing there and, as we waited, we all began to talk about the events of the day. He was a minister named Jim, from somewhere in New England and was also on his way home. As our van pulled up, I continued talking to him as the others boarded the van. I was the last one getting in when I asked him if he would like to take my place. He thanked me but said he was waiting for some friends who were picking him up. I piled in and we took off for Birmingham.

We had been on the road for a while when the driver turned on the radio to hear what was being reported about the march. We heard that a man had been badly beaten on a street corner in Selma. He was in serious condition, and was being transported to a Birmingham hospital A few minutes later an ambulance raced by us with siren blaring. We later realized that it must have been the one from Selma. We listened to the radio for more information only to learn that the man who had been beaten was Jim Reeb, the guy I had been talking to less than an hour before. We all said to one another, "There, but for the grace of God, go I." We prayed for him and continued toward the airport. It was later we heard that Jim had died. We were all deeply saddened as we boarded our flight to Atlanta. Had he taken my spot in that van, I might not be telling this story today.

Arriving at the airport, we said our good-bys to our Episcopal priest friend and headed for the ticket counter. My seat was next to a rabbi from Chicago. As we talked about Jim Reeb's death, I became aware of a deepening guilt. As I talked with the rabbi, I got in touch with the source of my guilt. I felt guilty to be alive. My seatmate noticed something going on with me, and I told him of my feelings of guilt. He said it was a common experience when people live through experiences in which others die. His words really spoke to my heart as he related incident after incident of many who had had a similar responses. He talked about many he had known who felt guilty for years for having survived the Holocaust. Though I never saw him again, his words helped calm my guilt.

As I deplaned in Chicago, I pulled out the last of my money to catch a taxi to our apartment behind the church in Evanston. It was late at night and Barbara greeted me with a sigh of relief and great hugs and kisses. She immediately told me she had seen me on the national news, recognizing my overcoat and walk. As she described where I was in the march I knew she had seen me. She then asked why my coat smelled so bad. I told her about the spitting and the debris that had been thrown at us and that I had not been able to shower in a couple of days. I thought the worst was over. The reality was my journey towards salvation was only beginning.

Chapter 3

HOME BUT NOT "AT HOME"

Barbara and I sat together in our upstairs bay window, overlooking the church parking lot. It was so good to be home; yet a lingering sadness accompanied me. I slept soundly and awoke late. I had received several calls so I decided to return them. Most of the calls were congratulatory, affirming what I had done. A couple of the calls were from church board members. They seemed cold toward my actions, not so much in what was said but in tone of voice and the questions they asked. One wanted to know who had given me the authority to go. Another wanted to know who paid for it. The questions sounded sinister, but I brushed that off as personal paranoia.

Over the next few days I went through an emotional, melancholy confusion. I remember sitting and staring out the bay window, letting my coffee get cold. Several times Barb asked if I was OK. I'd half-heartedly answer that I was. The truth was that I was trying to put together many events, not only of the past few days, but also of the last few years: people, national and local politics, work conversations, books I had read, magazine articles, school, Methodist church politics, meeting Edna Hutchins and, through her, hearing and meeting E. Stanley Jones.

Then there were the young people's groups, which had grown to almost forty in the senior high and twenty in the junior high. We had had several retreats and amazing experiences took place with these young people. We also were one of the few, perhaps the only, youth groups in our area that was, unconsciously, integrated. We never planned it; it just happened. We had Caucasians, African Americans, several

Native Americans and several Asian kids.

Other incidents came to mind that took place in the years leading up to Selma. I thought of the painter who fell off his chair in my office, then sat down in the chair across from me and began loudly repenting, even though I had not said a word. Then there were Phillip and Johnny, who tearfully thanked me for revealing the reality of God in Jesus. I had done nothing and really didn't know what they were talking about. These sovereign events puzzled me and caused me further confusion.

On Saturday I received a telephone call from an Evanston attorney. He was deeply involved in the civil rights movement and pushing for open-housing legislation in Evanston. He had heard of my recent Selma trip and invited me to share my experience at a large meeting of supporters. The meeting was to present a civil petition for the open-housing legislation to be put on an upcoming ballot. They hoped to get many signatures of support and then publish it in the local papers as well as getting radio and TV coverage. He said several hundred influential people from the black and white communities would attend the dinner and that I would be the keynote speaker. Even though I was flattered, I was also apprehensive. Still, I agreed to accept the invitation.

That Sunday before the service the head of the church board confronted me. "You had no business being an agitator from the north, going where you were neither welcomed nor wanted. Furthermore, who do you think you are to be so certain of the rightness of this 'black-commie's cause?" He went on to say that as the assistant minister of our church I had been a bad example to the youth I was supposed to be leading, even though all of the youth had been very proud of me. His final word was that I represented a minority viewpoint in our church. As such, I was giving our church a bad name, all of which would be brought up in the next official board meeting. At that time I would be severely dealt with.

After this public dressing down, several people came over to praise and encourage me. I entered that Sunday morning service frightened, confused, and lonely. The head pastor said little to me except to remind me that I should have gotten the Board's permission to go to Selma and not have acted so independently righteous. Already wobbly inside, I began second-guessing myself.

I didn't know if anyone would even come to that evening's youth group meeting. I was certain that the parents were really upset with me and would forbid the kids to come. However, at the early afternoon meeting with the junior high, there were about a third more students than usual. They all wanted to know about my trip, with all the details. Stunned, I told them all I could remember. At the end, several asked if they could stay and meet with the older group also.

About an hour or so later the seniors began to flood in, excited to hear from me. They, too, wanted to know every detail and talk about what was going on in the church and in the community concerning racism. There must have been at least fifty or sixty kids there. I shared my story and then they asked questions. We talked for over an hour and a half about what they should do to get involved. Many of them, whatever their race, expressed that their parents were really concerned about my trip and the integrated youth group we had. Many of their parents believed nothing good would come of it, and we would only stir up the status quo and cause dissention in the church, school, and the community at large. Several, both white and black, expressed that their parents were concerned about inter-racial dating. They were cautioning their children that if society kept moving in this direction, pretty soon there would be nothing to stop the eventual mixing of the races, and neither race wanted that.

What the kids talked about that afternoon and evening was extremely profound. They spontaneously prayed for their families, themselves, our city, and our nation as well as for me.

They asked God to help me stand up the next night at the open housing meeting. I went home that night buoyed in heart and soul. I slept much better, attended some school classes I was taking on Monday, and came home to prepare for the evening meeting. Despite the positive experience with the kids the day before, I still had a deep haunting in my heart. Something ominous was going on, but I wasn't in touch with what it could be.

As Barbara and I ate dinner that evening with our daughter, Becky, Barb encouraged me not to worry or be too concerned. She reminded me that all I had to do was to tell the truth and "let the chips fall where they may." She was a great comfort. It was only after an early dinner with my family that I remembered that the open-housing meeting was also to start with a dinner. Trying to calm my apprehensions, off I went!

Chapter 4

THE REAL PROBLEM

THE EVENING STARTED amicably enough. After eating and friendly chatting with several other folks, both black and white, the dishes were cleared and the meeting began. A black minister, who was evidently the Master of Ceremonies, introduced a white lawyer, who quoted a scripture from one of the Minor Prophets. He read from the book of Micah, "*He has told you, Oh, man, what is good: And what does the Lord require of you but to do justice, to love kindness, and to walk humbly with your God.*" He made a few comments about the legal action they were initiating and hoped everyone would sign the prepared open-housing petition. He then gave the meeting back to the emcee.

His introduction of me made me sound so noble and heroic, I couldn't help but blush. As the man heaped praise upon me, I thought to myself, "If only he knew how inadequate and frightened I had been through most of that time, his words would have been much less flattering." When he had finished his lengthy introduction, I rose to speak.

Initially, I felt overwhelmed with the responsibility to communicate as faithfully and truthfully as possible. I began by recounting the factors leading up to my decision to go to Selma. I followed with a blow-by-blow account of the march itself. The crowd was enthusiastic and responsive. They drew far more from me than I ever anticipated. I ended up talking for at least forty-five minutes. When I finally stopped, the MC as well as the crowd joined in sustained, vigorous applause with a few loud whistles thrown in.

The over the top praises continued as the agenda moved forward toward its climax, the signing of the open-housing petition. Many realtors would not show black families homes in generally non-black areas. He also said that there were fear tactics used by realtors on whites; that if they let a black family in their neighborhoods, they would have an immediate drop in property values. Despite that, I recalled my many conversations with black co-workers who told me that some black realtors had been in cahoots with white realtors to fan the flames of racial hatred. Unethical business practices were not necessarily racial but simply human. As the crowd began to mingle and chat together, he handed the petition to me. As I began to read the petition, the emcee said, "You don't have to read it. Just sign it!"

"Oh, I'm going to sign it! I just want to read it first." I assured him.

He then roughly grabbed the petition and said, "Listen, Whitey, just sign the f.... petition, for Christ's sake!"

As I turned to face him, a numbing shock of recognition passed through me like a laser beam. There, in front of me, in that man's eyes was the same hatred that I'd seen in the white faces lining the streets of Selma. The distended veins in the throat, the snake-like eyes, and the volcanic hostility were all too familiar! For a brief moment, I was back in Selma. I was speechless.

Having taken the petition from me, he now pushed it back at me, wanting me to hurry up because there wasn't much time. I signed it and passed it on. Then he spoke again, "There now, that wasn't so hard; was it, Whitey?"

I mumbled, "No," and shakily rose to leave.

I was glad to see him follow the petition around the room. I tried to be as inconspicuous as possible as I searched for the exit. Still dazed and shaken, I made it to the door and to my car after about twenty minutes of fending off more complimentary comments. I opened the door, got in, and locked the doors. As I sat down, my heart raced. My hands and forehead were cold and clammy. I knew something was going on that my mind could not quite catch up with. Stunned, I just sat there, motionless. It was ten minutes or so until I could start the engine and slowly make my way back to our apartment.

Barbara could immediately see that something was quite wrong. "So...what happened?"

I searched for words to explain the life-altering process going on in my soul. "Honey, do you remember when the cartoon character Jerry would hit Tom, and the cat would just disintegrate?"

"Yes?" She waited for more.

"That has just happened to me. Everything I have ever believed about God, life, injustices, church, the meaning of existence, and the very motivation for living has just died." Before me marched humanity of all colors, all equal regarding their capacity for hatred and cruelty. The problem wasn't just racial, it was human. I had been so naïve. I began to feel the weight of the political, emotional, and theological baggage I had been carrying. I was not only naïve, but also, absolutely, without hope. With despair verging on terror, I discovered I had been willing to give my life for a false fix. Civil rights, as noble as they were, were not going to solve the injustices or the long-standing racial inequity. The sand on which I had been standing shifted beneath my feet, and I was face-down in a swamp of desolation.

Little by little, the implications of this new insight were reinforced by past memories. Martin Luther King had acknowledged that laws don't change people's hearts. I recalled other conversations with my black friends at the Board. They resented liberal whites who looked upon them as projects. They felt patronized and that they were being used to salve the conscience of the white community. Another past conversation revealed the prejudices among blacks themselves; the communal distrust of any conservative, educated, and successful black man who was often labeled an Uncle Tom or a Whitey, servants of "THE MAN!" The overarching premise justifying these divisions was coming into bold relief and was this: all blacks or other minorities are intrinsically noble, while all whites are unethical and devious.

This premise had become the justification for the violence and hatred promoted by the Black Panthers, Black Muslims, and other hate groups of the 60's. This had also motivated the political divisions between the races. No wonder I generated surprise and disbelief when my black friends discovered I was a Goldwater Republican. How could I be for social justice, racial and economic equality and vote for Goldwater? Even I was baffled.

The God whom I was about to meet had effectively smashed the idol of social justice in my heart. He was getting ready to reveal Himself to me as the only One Who can deal with the dark wickedness in every human heart, most importantly, my own. Little did I know that my pilgrimage after reality was about to take me into one of the darkest places of my life. But before we go there, let's look back and see what else God had done to prepare me to become one who would come to love and follow Him.

Chapter 5

THE PULPIT

GOD FIRST SPOKE to me when I was 9 years old. I had gone downtown on the Kenmore bus to the Court Street Church for Wesley Boys' Choir rehearsal, a weekly ritual. Arriving around 3:45, all the boys and I ran through the huge church until Mr. Farley yelled for us to begin at 4:00.

I remember the large sanctuary very well. Its altar area had two choir lofts, each facing the other, with five rows for the choirs that would be singing that week. Next to one of the choir lofts was a huge pipe organ. I remember thinking that God must surely be pleased with how loud it sounded.

Next to the opposite loft was the pulpit. It had three huge steps going up to it, as it poked out into the sanctuary, like the prow of a great sailing ship. It always remained dark until the minister stepped in to give his sermon. When he did, the main lights would go down and all attention would be on the pulpit.

For a young boy, that was a scary time in the service. I can remember thinking: "Can I leave to go pee?" Or would that make God mad; but if not God, at least my dad. And did God know about peeing? I knew that getting up and going would cause scowls and grimaces, so I always tried my best to wait until the service was over.

There was a large semi-circle of pews downstairs and a similar semi-circle balcony, where my family always sat, in the same pew every week. Dad always sat on the end, then Mom, then my four-year older brother, Jack. Jack's main joy in life was the daily harassment of his younger brother, me, a job he excelled at.

Downstairs, there was a large room behind the sanctuary where the choirs practiced. There were seven choirs in all, and over time, except for the Wesley girls' choir, I sang in them all. After a seemingly endless rehearsal, I left the choir room to wait for my dad, who would pick me up on his way home. I always dreaded the wait, especially in winter, as it could get very cold. Many times I remember it being zero or below. On this particular Wednesday, Mr. Farley had to leave earlier than usual and asked if I would make sure the large main door was shut. He said it would automatically lock as I pushed it shut. Knowing how cold it was, he said I could wait inside, out of the cold, until my dad pulled up in front to get me.

After practice, he left along with all my fellow singers. I was alone behind that huge door. I remember my mother telling me that Dad would be a little later than usual. I looked out the door and the wind almost blew it shut, catching me between the door and the doorpost. I struggled to get free and let the door close. I stood inside, much warmer, in this place behind the big door called the Narthex. I knew that because, from time to time, we boys would be asked to go into the Narthex and jump on the rope that hung from the ceiling and ring the bell in the tower. Many fights broke out over who got to do this. The fights usually took place on the steps we had to climb and jump off to grab the bell rope. Ultimately, Mr. Farley would have to separate us and choose one or two to do the deed. As I stood in the silence, I contemplated whether or not I should jump up and ring the bell without permission. I decided against it. All downtown would hear and I would be in big trouble.

As I stood there, waiting, I stretched up on my tiptoes and peeked through the glass in the door that led into the sanctuary. All was dark except for the "eternal light" that hung down from the four-story ceiling, glowing ominously. I opened the door and stepped into the singly lit sanctuary. I had the sense that a great adventure was about to begin. I moved slowly into the cavernous room and started down the aisle, cautiously at first, certain someone might see me. I was especially worried that God would see me in His Room. I slowly walked further down the aisle, courage, excitement and fear building with every step. Working my way down the aisle, I finally came to the first row of pews on the west side. It was only then that I looked up, and saw it. There, towering over me, like the prow of a great sailing ship, was The Pulpit.

It looked a mile high. I thought, for just an instant, that even being there might constitute a transgression, or at the very least, a trespassing on private property of some kind. Having come this far, however, I thought, why not go for it, and see what the whole place looks like from up there. Looking each way before moving, I quietly moved on tiptoe. Coming to the base of the stairs and taking a deep breath, I began the ascent. Slowly I climbed up about six or seven steps until I came to the place where there was a sharp right turn and saw the last three huge steps up to the top. There I stood, so far so good.

I looked up and saw the Eternal Red Light, suspended from the high ceiling above me. It gave an eerie, almost Halloweenish glow so nothing could really be clearly seen. In fact, the sanctuary seemed full of shadows. I felt strangely cold. I shivered, looked around again, and took the first of the three steps. All was silent. My weight shifted onto the step and nothing happened. Emboldened, I stepped onto the second. Finally, with a burst of nine year old courage, I reached the third and last step. As I did, it squeaked. My heart leaped into my mouth, and I could feel my chest pounding. I soon realized it was just the noise from the step. I grabbed one side of The Pulpit and stood there, frozen, until my heart returned to its normal pace.

As I waited, I suddenly remembered that my dad was

coming soon. I had to be outside waiting for him so that he
didn't have to come looking for me. I was now torn in a time
constraint, wanting to stand fully upright in The Pulpit and take
in the view, yet, also wanting to be in the right place for Dad.

I quickly formed my plan: I would turn and step directly
behind the lectern, peer over for a brief look, then quickly
descend the stairs, run up the aisle and out the door and be
there waiting for Dad when he arrived. Feeling fully confident,
I turned and stepped up to the lectern. Suddenly the whole
place lit up. As I looked up, all I saw was a blinding light.
I thought I would surely die on the spot. Just then the stair
squeaked and my heart leapt, my chest pounded, and the
hair stood up on the back of my head. Instantly, my face was
drained of blood, and a fear of wetting my pants enveloped
me. God had caught me, and I was in big trouble. I was in the
"forbidden" place; I was in "The Pulpit." Only God knew what
was going to happen next. I tried to move but was glued to the
spot. All of life stopped. The world was over. I prepared to die.

How long I stood, transfixed, I don't know: a few seconds,
a few minutes? I do remember that I was too afraid to even turn
my head or wiggle my toes. Eventually blood began to return
to my face, and more regular heartbeats thumped a lessening of
my fear. As I was beginning to sense some form of normalcy, I
became aware of something under my left foot, like an acorn,
or something hard. Hesitatingly, I turned my head downward,
and slowly lifted my foot, revealing a small shiny button-like
looking thing there on the floor. I wondered what it could be.
Bending down to look more closely, I saw that it was a metal
switch of some sort, sticking up through the floor. I bent further
down, and, touching it ever so carefully, I gently pushed it. All
of a sudden the room went dark.

Oh no! I thought I had broken whatever it was and might
be in even bigger trouble. Hastily, I pushed the button again
and, "Behold!" the bright light returned. I instantly received a
revelation. The button was a light switch. I excitedly began to

push it on and off. Light, dark. Light, dark. "Hey," I thought, "this is fun!"

No sooner had my delight about this discovery dawned than I realized how it all worked on Sunday when the other lights got dim and there was light on "The Pulpit." Why, there was nothing mysterious about it after all. It was nothing God was doing; it was something the minister himself did. Imagine that!

At this juncture an event took place which, to this day, I do not fully understand. Standing there in that great pulpit, I felt the most peaceful and pleasant I had ever felt before. I felt that I belonged there, that somehow this was what I was created for. In that moment, all fear left, and I was filled with the greatest joy I had ever experienced. I began to speak out something about God to an imaginary audience. To this day I have no idea what I said. All I know was that God, whoever and wherever He was, was as thrilled as I was, maybe even more.

I began to cry tears from someplace inside me I didn't know existed. I jumped up and down on the button with delight and laughter. Then I just stood there; I can't remember for how long. Soon, smiling from ear to ear, I methodically and without any fear descended from The Pulpit. For a nine year old boy something holy, private, mysterious, and awesome had occurred; something that for a few moments seemed to defy time and space.

As I rather regally walked back up the aisle, I knew something had happened deep inside me that I would never forget. I pushed through the sanctuary door and headed through the narthex to the huge front door. I felt very warm, even looking forward to a cold December afternoon. I slammed the huge door shut and heard the lock click. Just as I did, Dad drove up and I ran to get in the car.

Jumping into the front seat, he asked why I was so smiley and happy. I thought for a moment and then said I really didn't know, but perhaps it was just because I could go skating in the back yard when we got home. That seemed to satisfy him, so I let it go at that. We talked of other things that night on the way home, of school, sports, even choir, and whether we were going to sing the next Sunday. I don't recall much else except that I didn't feel guilty about not telling him what had happened. It was a secret between me and a God who was waiting to come to me in much greater fullness.

Chapter 6

WHAT JESUS DOESN'T DO ANYMORE

Most kids raised in a church situation have from time to time been faced with DVBS—Daily Vacation Bible School. It usually comes for at least two weeks in the summer and came for me practically every year. However there was one year that would impact me deeply for the next 20. My mother had volunteered to help, as was her practice, so, I, of course, was enrolled. I never did understand why my brother never once, that I recall, attended one single summer session. Being four years older he seemed to be exempt from many things.

 This particular DVBS must have been in 1944 or 45. The programs consisted of all sorts of Bible oriented themes, crafts, coloring, pasting, eating box lunches, and, my favorite activity, singing. Our daily teacher was a kind, sweet, white-haired lady that all the kids liked. She had a soft voice and was quite patient and respectful toward us.

About halfway through the second week we were coloring pictures. Staying inside the lines was always a great struggle for me, a trait that also carried over into my life in general. That particular day, however, I did reasonably well. I really enjoyed the Bible stories that were the basis of the coloring projects.

On the morning in question we had just heard the story of Jesus and the healing of the blind man Bartimeaus. As we were all coloring our pictures of the healing scene, our teacher talked a little more about the story. As she talked a question came to my mind. I innocently raised my hand to get her attention. When she called my name I excitedly asked where Jesus might still be doing the kinds of things we were reading about. I thought I would really like to see things like that, and hadn't seen such things happen at our church. Along with my first question, I asked at the same time if we all couldn't go this week and see where Jesus was working like that.

The rest of the kids in the class picked up on it and chimed in, agreeing that that would be a great field trip. As we all began to talk and speculate, our teacher tried to get some order back in the class. When she finally regained some control she said, to me, "Tommy, Jesus doesn't do things like that anymore. Now we have doctors!"

While she said it in the kindest, most grandmotherly way possible, in that moment a great sadness bordering on instant tears overwhelmed me. I felt so sorry for Jesus and His Father, God. Did she mean that doctors replaced God and Jesus? I was too sad to ask any more questions. I couldn't speak. I was so sorry that God and Jesus didn't do things like that anymore.

I'm sure my well meaning teacher had no idea how her answer affected me and, perhaps, others. She was giving the best she had. I only know that it would be another 20 or so years before I would ever truly believe in God again. I would continue to attend church with my family, be involved in youth group, sing in the choirs, etc. But my belief that there was really a God of power, miracles, and love, who could be known and with whom you could have a relationship, became submerged that day. It would take some very cataclysmic events to open the door to once again hoping there really was a God and that He was like Jesus and could be known.

Chapter 7

RETROSPECTIVE REVELATION

Going Through the Windshield with God

THERE ARE POINTS in our lives when we can only see the hand of God by looking backward. We did not know he was with us then, but looking through the lens of time, there are many instances in our lives where God was surely with us, looking out for us, preparing and protecting us for what would eventually come. This is one of those times.

Cold is the word that describes winter in northern Illinois. It was especially cold the night of January 22, 1952. At ten degrees above zero it was perfect with the sky clear as the proverbial bell. My buddies and I had come from a movie and had gathered at Bruce's house to decide what to do.

We decided since we had a TV at our house, we would all pile into Bruce's dad's car and drive to my house to watch some TV. The 1940's vintage Dodge churned over a few times before finally firing up. We waited a few minutes for it to warm up and then all piled in. The old Dodge had one of those windshields that was divided by a metal post. Fred sat on the outside of the front seat with me in the middle and Bruce driving. In the back seat were my other buddies, Kenny and Dick. As we left Bruce's house we commented on how slick and reflective the streets were. My house was about three miles away so, having called my Dad to tell him he was about to be invaded, we started out.

As Bruce drove toward my house, we were laughing and

poking each other. Bruce was obviously having some difficulty with traction. The street was like glass. We went about two miles when, coming down Custer Avenue, the ice sheet we were driving on caused the car to career out of control. We slid across the road directly into a tree. Bruce hit the steering wheel hard and passed out. Fred sitting next to me in the front seat, bounced off the windshield, breaking it and receiving a deep cut in his throat. We were later to find out that the cut had gone all the way to the carotid artery, exposing it but not cutting it.

I went directly through the windshield taking out the center post. My knees caught on the dashboard, stopping my forward progress and dragging me back across the jagged edges of the broken glass. In the back seat, Kenny and Dick had been roughed up also, smashing into the front seat and hurting both knees and their heads. Bruce and I were hurt the worst, along with Fred who was bleeding profusely.

I can only remember that a lady whose house was on the corner gave me a towel to blot up the blood from the cuts in my face. I was in shock. I recall trying to look into a mirror and not being able to track what was going on. The next thing I remember was an ambulance ride where, on and off, I could hear the siren and the medics talking as they tried to stop the flow of blood. I recall being in the emergency room and yelling at the doctor to stop pushing my eyes out.

I later found out that Dr. Quandt, who was our family physician and tended to my wounds, had been in the Second World War as a combat surgeon. He had seen it all on the battlefields of Europe and was truly qualified to deal with my situation.

While I was in the hospital, I had an intense dream. The dream was of a beautiful blue puffy sky. In the middle of the sky something small kept moving closer and closer. After a few moments I could begin to discern that it was wooden. Soon it came into view and I recognized it as a cross. Quickly it came toward me and soon filled my whole vision. Instantly I woke up. It was 18 hours after the accident and amazingly I was fairly clear headed, lying in a hospital room.

I soon realized that someone was across the room from me. It was Bruce. He lay there with no shirt on and his chest painted bright orange. The first thing he said was, "Tom you are the ugliest guy I have ever seen; you ought to try out for the next Frankenstein movie!" He went on a little more, making me laugh. Soon I felt blood trickling down my chin. The nurse came running in and called for the doctor. He redid two stitches and told me not to talk or laugh for awhile.

Quickly I began to remember the events of the night before. I found out that the other guys had been treated and released from the hospital. Bruce told me that he had had some sort of a previous lung condition that could only be treated by collapsing one lung. This had happened in the accident and now he only had to let the lung return to its normal place and he would be much better.

Right after this my parents came in and we cried together, thankful that I was alive. I had lost so much blood there were some concerns for my recovery. Later that evening some of my high school buddies came up to see us. They told me that a couple of girls had wanted to come in and see me but had caught a glance of my face and had vomited. I learned also that the tip of my nose had been cut off and one of the guys had brought it to the hospital where Dr. Quandt had sewn it back on. I further learned that I had 112 double stitches in my face alone, with some other less serious bruises, and cuts.

Several days went by with a lot of visitors coming. About ten or so days later I was released from the hospital and went home to recuperate. My doctor told me that it would be good for me both physically and psychologically if I would go back to school as soon as possible so my friends and teachers could see the improvement from the swelling and the stitches. I wasn't too happy at the prospect, remembering that some of the girls had thrown up at the sight of me. I also remembered the first time I held a mirror and looked at myself. Bruce was right there, preparing me for the shock of my first look. As I looked at myself he said I could tell girls that these were dueling scars and, therefore were signs of great bravery and courage and that I should be proud of them. His constant comments and humor helped me in ways I still don't understand.

As I contemplated returning to school I was filled with apprehension. My first day back was a Friday and there was a sock hop that night. My buddies said if I didn't go they would come and get me. I made it through the school day with a minimum of stares and looks, but as I thought about the dance that night, I was quite anxious. While getting ready for the dance, I recall glancing in the mirror and then avoiding it. I reached for my faithful Old Spice and turning my back to the mirror, I dashed it on my face, enduring the stinging and thought to myself, "Well at least I'll smell good."

Pete came to pick me up. He literally pulled me into his car set me down and told me we were going.

When we arrived the dance was already in full swing. I walked through the cafeteria door, where the dance was held, and, as soon as I was inside, a young lady named Bobbie greeted me. She was a cheerleader, the homecoming queen and my first high school crush. Smiling she took my hand and led me to the dance floor. It was a slow dance and sensing my hesitancy and shock, she put my arms around her. She then, very tenderly, laid her head on my chest and pressed close to me and relaxed into the dance. As I look back on this event,

I am absolutely certain that a young sixteen-year-old boy was healed of fears that could have haunted him for a lifetime. All fear drained away as we danced that dance. I wonder if she ever knew what she did for me that night.

Fifty one years later, in September 2003, Barbara and I attended my 50th high school reunion. It was the first one I had been to and I eagerly desired to see many of my old classmates. One person I especially hoped to see was Bobbie as I had not seen her since graduation. Sadly I learned that she had died several years earlier. Though I was sorry that I never had the chance to tell her what a gift she had given to a very frightened young boy, I could look back and thank God for all the kindnesses shown to me throughout that whole ordeal. Though I didn't know him yet, the Lord had his eyes on me.

Chapter 8

LEARNING LIFE LESSONS

Joe: Building a Better Manhole

AFTER HIGH SCHOOL I enlisted in the Army. That was an experience I look back on with no sense of pride. I spent a good amount of time in Philippine bars drunkenly wrapped around a bottle of beer and singing choruses. Oddly enough, the one I repeated the most had to do with how the Lord needed to forgive my sins and set me free. In God's providence that was a precursor of what was to come later on.

I was discharged in 1957 and upon arriving home needed a job. My uncle Ted was the city engineer for the City of Rockford and recommended I try and get on with a work crew that graded and laid out streets in new developments. I soon found myself working as a day laborer for a local contractor. Through this connection I met a man I'll call Joe. Joe was an Italian and his family had immigrated to America while he was in his teens. He had an Italian accent and was a great guy. So I found it difficult to understand why my fellow workers disliked Joe so much. In fact, they hated him. I worked with him daily and soon began to notice something different about him.

He was a hard worker and although quiet seemed to cause problems with the other workers. I heard them talking about him all the time with great resentment. I couldn't understand this. He never spoke ill of or offended anyone. He was the first to work in the morning. He took only the 15-minute breaks the union contract outlined. He only took ½ hour breaks for lunch, and didn't stop work until the foreman said to.

I searched for an answer in conversations with the guys and their comments were: "He's just a brown nose," or "You know these 'Dagos' they aren't too smart;" or He's a religious nut a 'mackerel snapper' (a rude euphemism for a Roman Catholic). They said he was bad for the union. I even felt some of their wrath as I would work and eat with Joe.

What I only later understood was that he set such a high standard of work ethic and faithfulness, he made the other union workers look lazy. Some of the union stewards didn't like Joe because he would refuse to slow down a job to prolong it. He also never complained about working conditions, or even wages. He was always cheerful, helpful and would take some of the dirtier jobs without a blink of the eye. He had a family whom he dearly loved and was a daily communicant at St. Anthony's Church in Rockford.

I had only worked on this job for several weeks when my uncle told me to apply for a city job that would pay more. I applied and became a city inspector. The job consisted of making sure that the specifications of the city contracts were met. These contracts were in new sub-divisions for roads and sewer drainage. Underground sewer pipe was laid as well as manholes were constructed. These were at intersections so that later if there were problems not only with sewer lines but also telephone and some electric lines, access could be had. These manholes were completely underground.

I soon was out in the sub-divisions again only this time as a city inspector. It wasn't long before I ran into Joe and the crew I had worked with. They greeted me with tolerance but also with some disdain. Joe however was genuinely happy to see me and we shared lunch together that same day. I noticed afresh the way the other workers treated him and once again was concerned and wondered why he was so vilified. Mind you, the foreman loved Joe and seemed to protect his job. This also caused problems, as the foreman was management not union.

As I went from job to job, I would occasionally see Joe. He always greeted me with the same warmth and joy. I saw many other crews and soon found there was quite a difference in the quality of work, especially in the building of manholes. I noticed that when manholes were to be built on Joe's crew the foreman always asked him to do it. This infuriated the other workers but Joe would build them, whistling and singing in Italian as he did. This really irritated the other workers. Joe was unfazed and went about building the most beautiful manholes. He would carefully lay each brick and clean the mortar off. He checked the level so that when he was done they were clean inside and wouldn't be filled with debris or water if one had to descend into them and work.

Other manholes I saw were slopped together, with mortar all over the place, the grades had to be checked and re-checked as it seemed they tried to get away with the sloppiest job they could. There was a mad rush to get these manholes covered up as quickly as possible. Often I would have to tell them to redo the job, and their anger sometimes was frightening. I never had a single problem with Joe's manholes. He would finish and call the foreman over who would then call me to inspect it. They looked like the outside of a new brick house. Then, and only then, would Joe cover up the manhole and move on to the next job. I wondered why Joe did such excellent work but it wasn't until a month or so later I was to find out.

As an engineer, my dad had laid out many sub-divisions for underground cable and telephone boxes. He knew many of the linemen from the telephone and electric companies who worked in manholes. Their quality was especially important when the linemen had to work in rainy or flooded conditions. Working in poorly constructed manholes meant that the water could be a foot deep in them. On those cold winter days a worker really appreciated a dry manhole. My dad told me that many linemen after an unusually hard cold day would come back to the garage and ask if anyone had worked in one of Joe's manholes. Those who did would tell with joy if they had. All throughout the city, linemen from the utility companies, as well as city workers would extol the "manholes of Joe." I later met some of those linemen. Every last one of them knew of Joe and loved him. They each seemed to have a bad weather story to tell about how grateful they had been to have had a manhole built by Joe.

When I saw Joe again I told him what I had heard about his manholes. He almost blushed as he thanked me. I asked him why he worked the way he did. He very softly said, "Joe doesn't work for the contractors or the city. Joe builds manholes for Jesus. Jesus must approve every manhole, and I am happy when He does." The sweetness of his broken English made his testimony even dearer to me. What's the point? Long before I became a Christian I had the testimony of a man who dearly loved Jesus and wanted his work ethic to show that. As a result, underneath many sub-divisions in the city of Rockford, Illinois, is a beautiful buried testimony hidden from man but known to God. I only hope that the work of my life has also led to many beautiful foundations being laid for Christ in the hearts of those we have the privilege to serve.

Chapter 9

EVANSTON MIRACLES

Wʜᴀᴛ ɪs ᴀ miracle? To my mind, a miracle is simply God doing something marvelous. To call what happened to Barbara and me in 1964 miracles is the only way I know to explain a series of events that would eventually change our lives.

Barbara and I had met in 1960 when I was working at NBC in Rockford, Illinois. One day after work, Bob, one of the on air personalities, asked me if I would be interested in trying out for a role in The Philadelphia Story, a play he was directing at the local Jewish Community Center. I thought a moment and said yes. The night of tryouts I watched as people auditioned for parts. Several had auditioned when a young blond girl with a pony tail auditioned for the role of the younger sister. I looked at her and quite suddenly and totally out of character I turned to Bob and said what I had never before said about anyone in my life. "Bob that is the girl I'm going to marry."

When I found out she was engaged to a Jewish folk singer, I felt sorry for the man as I was sure she would be mine. I did have to do some courting, to be sure. But to my continuing joy, a little over a year later we were married on April 22, 1961. Our daughter, Rebecca, was born in December of that year, the first of what would become a large and rambunctious set of kids.

Barb and I decided it would be a good thing to raise our family in church although, at that time, neither one of us had had an experience with God. We had been attending church since our marriage. Having deep admiration for our local Methodist minister, I thought the ministry might be a desirable profession. I talked with him and took some tests which seemed to suggest that a career in serving people would be well suited for me. These personality and vocational tests indicated that my abilities would also be well suited for the legal profession or psychology or a counseling career. My highest scores were in social work of some kind.

Armed with this knowledge, Barb and I decided that I should go back to college and prepare for the ministry. The test scores indicated this would be the profession that best covered my strengths. The Methodist church had a saying on its letterhead from the department for potential ministers that read, "Where the line of your abilities crosses the line of the world's need, there is God's call for you." Later on I would come to have real problems with this view. However, after talking to our minister, we decided that Kendall Jr. College, in the heart of Northwestern University and close to Garrett Seminary, would be an ideal place to resume my education.

I already had about two years of college credit in Physical Education, some at The University of Illinois, both before and after my three years in the Army. The fact is, I had treated school as a lark and, though passing some courses, had basically blown off my studies. I later attended school in Lacrosse, Wisconsin; but after one semester, I left and went to California with a buddy, returning home about a year later. On that trip, I met Frank Sinatra and Dean Martin in Las Vegas; but that's a story for another day.

Now married and trying to settle down, Barb and I realized

if I were going to go back to school, we would have to move to Evanston, Illinois, and that she might have to work to help me through school. I had hoped to get my G.I. Bill reinstated, but knew I would also have to work to get through school. We decided I should spend a day in Evanston and find out what it would take for me to get back into school.

One very cold January morning in 1962, I went into Evanston to try to accomplish three things: to get accepted in school, to find a place to live, and to get a job. That was a pretty big order for one day, but we didn't know any better at that time. We lived about 90 miles from Evanston. I left around 5 A.M. The outside temperature was zero. As I crossed the river and drove out East State Street toward the toll way, I wondered if I wasn't really a bit crazy. Me, a minister! Who would believe that?

I paid my toll and headed out that cold, bright, sunny day. Everything seemed so still along the road, like the world was frozen. The rising sun was glorious. I had to squint to see the road ahead. I had passed the exit to Elgin and had driven perhaps a mile or two further when the strangest thing happened.

There was little traffic on the road in either direction, and I had a feeling of isolation. It was a feeling of being closed in and, yet, being watched. It was eerie and exciting at the same time. I was clearly awake when I noticed about a mile down the toll way that the end of a beautiful full rainbow had settled down on a large out-building of a farm. At the same time, across the road, I saw the other end of the same rainbow, just as brilliant and full. It filled a small grove of trees with luminous colors. Then, in an instant, the rest of the arching part of the rainbow appeared. It was as if someone had gently placed the two ends of it down first and then placed the middle part onto the two colorful posts.

It stretched over the highway and I could see the whole

thing. It was a full, beautiful rainbow with colors I could not even begin to describe. As I drove nearer, I felt as though I was going to pass through a colorful tunnel, as it seemed to come closer to the sides of the toll way, as well as diminish in height. The colors were brilliant. They never changed as I approached. Within 30 to 45 seconds the rainbow was on both sides of the car and moving right along with it. It seemed that perhaps another 30-45 seconds passed, with the rainbow and the car just moving along together. Soon, however, the rainbow was only on my side of the toll way. I was about to freak out when the colors swarmed into the car filling it up like a kaleidoscope. There were colors of all kinds, filling the interior of the car, cascading back and forth across the dashboard and windshield. I was shaking, wondering what the hell was going on. I couldn't hear the car engine at all but I remember clutching the steering wheel for dear life. This lasted for another 30-45 seconds and then, instantly, it disappeared. I remember wondering how could there be such a rainbow on such a clear day. To say that I was befuddled is an understatement. I had never seen such a clear rainbow in my life, either after or during a rainstorm.

But there was much more to come.

Chapter 10

ARRIVING IN EVANSTON

I SLOWLY REGAINED my senses, even though they had been on overload. I looked around to see if anyone else was on the toll road, going in either direction, that might also have seen the rainbow; but I was utterly alone, not a car in sight as far as I could see. My heartbeat slowly returned to normal, but it must have taken about 15 minutes. Only then did I begin to think about what had happened. As I thought about the incident, I became deeply aware of a joy and confidence concerning my trip. It was as though I knew something before any of it had happened, and that everything was going to be fine, so I could just sit back and enjoy the trip.

I soon found my way to Evanston and Kendall Junior College. Pulling up in front of the school, I noticed it wasn't open. I parked right in front and left the motor running to stay warm, as I wondered what might happen next.

Barbara later told me that after I left she had been awakened and had prayed for God's help. For her this was a first; crying out to God in a way that surprised even her. As I sat in the car, pondering the morning's events and the emotion that coursed through me, I somehow knew everything was going to be all right. All I had to do was walk through the doors that would be opened for me. It was as if I had intelligence from another source and I needed to heed it. I also knew I was free to disregard it if I wanted to. I was choosing to follow these emotions when a car pulled up behind me. A distinguished man in his late fifties or early sixties got out. He nodded and proceeded to the front door of the College, opening the door and going in.

Soon afterwards, the lights went on, and he returned to unlock the front door. Only then did he acknowledge me and gesture for me to come in. I quickly shut off the car and bounced up the sidewalk as he graciously held the door open for me, put out his hand, and said, "It sure is cold this morning, isn't it?" I responded affirmatively. He went on to tell me he would have a cup of coffee for both of us in a few minutes. I sat down in the foyer as he went back into his office.

About five minutes later he poked his head out of his office door, asking if I needed cream or sugar. I said, "No," and soon he was walking out with two cups of steaming coffee. Sitting down beside me, he said his name was Wesley Westerberg. I introduced myself and proceeded to tell him why I was there. He seemed very interested and soon I was telling him about my desire to re-enter college, and that this time I wanted to learn something. He said he had met many older men and women coming back to school who had greater motivation for learning than younger students, especially those with a family. When I agreed, he invited me to come into his office. It was only then that I noticed on the door, "Dr. Wesley M. Westerberg, President."

He graciously offered me a seat and said he would love to help me out. I told him all I wished to accomplish in one day. That included getting accepted in school, getting a job and finding a place for my family to live. He smiled and said he thought that would be no problem at all. He gave me some papers to fill out concerning registration for the next semester, which was due to start in two weeks. He then looked through his file and directed me to go to the Methodist Board of Lay Activities and speak to a man there whom he knew. Afterward, I was to go to a certain address and see a man about a place to live. I filled out the papers and gave them to him, telling him I would return as soon as possible. He gave me directions for both places and bid me goodbye, saying he hoped to see me soon.

By this time it was well after 8 a.m. and I was on my way to the Board of Lay Activities. As I walked in, a man greeted me with a smile and another cup of coffee. I told him who had sent me and soon I was filling out a job application. He looked at it and said I could start as soon as I moved to Evanston. He also said he could work around any class schedule I might have. Then I left, saying to myself how easy that was.

I then drove to Forest Avenue, which was one block off Lake Michigan, a street of beautiful homes. I drove into the driveway of the address Dr. Westerberg had given me and knocked at the front door. An elderly man in his early seventies or so answered and invited me in. I told him my story and how I had gotten his name. He stood up, smiled, and said, "Come on. Let me show you something!"

We walked through his lovely home and out the back door where I saw a three-car garage with some upstairs windows. He opened the garage and we passed through an inside door which led to the stairs. These stairs led to a lovely apartment, with a big kitchen, two bedrooms, a full bath and a living room overlooking the driveway and back yard. It was partially furnished but he said that he would remove anything I didn't need if I wished to use my own furniture. He couldn't help noticing that I was stunned and standing there, speechless. After a few moments he asked if the apartment would work out for me. I said it was wonderful but I didn't know if I could afford it. He smiled and said that if I would take care of the yard and keep the place looking nice, I could have it rent free. He would even pay the utilities. He went on to say that he thought it might take eight to ten hours a week to keep it up, but that my studies must always come first.

I stood there numb, asking if I had heard him correctly. Unsure I had understood him, I repeated everything as I had heard it: eight to ten hours a week, keeping the lawn mowed and the beds weeded, watered, and cultivated and shoveling the snow in the winter. He assured me that was all, except that from time to time he might ask my wife to type some letters for him. That, however, wouldn't be often, and she would be able to spend her time taking care of the baby and me. He put out his hand and asked when I could move in. I said I hoped to be able to do so in about ten days, since school started in two weeks. He said, "Great!" and escorted me down the stairs and then down the driveway to my car. He told me to let him know when we would arrive so he could make sure the heat was on. I said I certainly would, and thanked him profusely as he waved and walked back into his house.

I sat momentarily in the driveway, shocked. I was to learn later that he was Harry Wells, the former Bursar of Northwestern University. He had also been head of the Quartermaster Corps in the First World War and was a leading member of a Methodist Church in Evanston. Harry Wells was well-known for his wisdom and generosity.

I drove slowly back to Kendall College, my head swirling at what had happened. I parked and made my way into the Administration Building. I sat down to gather my wits when a tall, middle-aged man with a kind looking face spotted me and asked if I was the Veteran who was wanting to get into school the next semester. I told him I was, indeed, a vet and I did want to get into school the next semester. He came over to the bench I was sitting on and grasped my hand. He lead me around the corner and into his office. The sign on the door read, "Dean of Admissions and Dean of Men." He stepped behind his desk and offered me another cup of coffee, which I gladly accepted. He looked over my admissions papers and, smiling, said, "Welcome to Kendall College. I look forward to getting to know both you and your wife."

I said, "You mean I'm accepted?"

"Yes," he said and immediately excused himself for a meeting he had to attend. All alone in his office, I sat back and considered my morning. A deep desire to cry for joy rose within me. I had to fight back the tears. What was going on, I asked myself. I looked at my watch and saw that it wasn't even 10:00 a.m.

As I finished my coffee and walked out of the office, a voice behind me called out, "Thomas, I hope everything has been worked out?" I turned and saw Dr. Westerberg. I assured him it certainly had and told him how grateful I was for his help. He smiled and waved goodbye. I got into my car and started the engine, amazed with what had happened. I was accepted in school. I had a job at a great wage. I had a beautiful apartment, rent and utility free. Now, all we had to do was move.

As I drove out of Evanston, I recalled all that had happened: the rainbow, the colors, Dr. Westerberg, the Dean, Mr. Wells, and my new boss at the Methodist Board of Lay Activities. Back home before noon, I tried to explain to Barbara all that had happened in so short a time. She listened excitedly. When I finished, she told me that a strange thing had happened to her, too. She told me about being awakened and praying with fierce sincerity. After her prayer, she had gone back to a sound sleep. After several hours she awoke with peace and joy, free from any anxiety about the future, school, or moving.

So began a journey that has gotten curiouser and curiouser, more and more fun, and more and more joyful over the years. It has been an adventure Barbara and I have enjoyed and continue to enjoy, right to these later years of our lives.

But before we would reach the heights of a true understanding of who Jesus really is, we would go through some dark valleys. You have already read about some of them from my journey to Selma. Following that event would come an even deeper low. But after the darkness comes the light. And Jesus was leading us on the path to our salvation.

Chapter 11

BAFFLED

Life settled into a whole new routine for us in Evanston. I attended seminary classes, Barb worked and we began to build life around being in ministerial service. I served as the youth pastor at a local Methodist church and began to have some speaking opportunities. Many of what to me were baffling occurrences took place during that time. The amazing thing is that neither of us were yet true believers.

Here are a few examples of those occurrences. The senior-high group I was working with had had some real encounters with God and with one another. It was after one of our retreats that the following happened. We had been to Peek Home, a former Methodist orphanage, for a retreat. There had been a presence of God among us that none of us could explain. After arriving home on Sunday night, two of the young men said they had to talk with me. I set up two early evening appointments for them to come to our apartment behind the church. The strange thing about these two stories is that they are almost identical.

The first young man came on Tuesday night. After some niceties, he and I went back to my little office. We had no sooner sat down than he looked at me and started crying. He told me that nothing was wrong; in fact, everything was wonderful. Confused, I asked some probing questions. He began by effusively thanking me for leading him to Christ. He then went on telling me about his previous doubts and questions about God, church, and where all of it fit into his life. He told me that over the past weekend he had literally met the living God and all his doubts were turning into opportunities to know reality. He said it was all because of Barbara and me.

I sat there, dumbfounded, wondering what we had done. I hadn't even talked with the kids about God in some way that could be construed as leading them to Christ. At that time neither Barbara nor I had become real Christians, so the boy's story made no sense to me. I listened as he detailed his revelations about knowing Jesus and being born again. I had never heard nor used that expression in my life. After about half an hour our talk ended and he went home.

The next evening I met with the second young man. His story of his experience with the Lord was almost identical. His thanks toward Barbara and I was just as profuse. When he left, I told Barbara about my times with the two boys. She was just as puzzled as I was. Nonetheless, we saw changes in those two young men's lives and their influence for Christ on the others in the Senior High Methodist Youth Fellowship. They really were changed and they never did stop thanking us.

Another incident involved the Parsonage Committee desiring to get our apartment painted. They told us that some painters would be by to look it over and give estimates. One Saturday morning a man in his mid-thirties came to the door, introduced himself, and told us he had been sent to give an estimate. He quickly looked through the apartment as I worked in my office.

Barb was in the kitchen right across from my office preparing lunch. The man came down the hall, walked into my office, which had no door, and plopped down in the chair behind me as I was working. I spun around, expecting to hear his estimate, when he literally fell off his chair onto his knees with a thud that made me think he must have hurt himself. He began to wail while trying to talk at the same time.

After about thirty seconds, with tears streaming down his cheeks, he gathered enough control that I could understand what he was saying. He poured out sin after sin: adultery, lying and cheating on painting jobs, using people, and his failure as a husband and father. He said life was hopeless and there was no way for him to undue all the damage he had done. Having trashed all his relationships, including the ones with his family, he was lost and without direction. He finally stopped after about ten minutes and asked me what he should do.

Barbara, who could hear everything from across the hall, and I had exchanged looks during his tirade. We were both completely caught off guard and at a total loss. I could only shrug my shoulders at her while he was carrying out his emotional catharsis. After he asked what he should do, I was dumbfounded and speechless.

Finally, after an embarrassing delay, I pathetically said, "Well, let's ask God." I bowed my head and opened my mouth to pray something. All of a sudden he began to pray like crazy. He told God all the stuff he had told me moments before and much more, detailing and telling God how sorry he was and pleading with God for forgiveness and another chance to live life.

I said nothing as he poured it all out. When he was done there was a long pause and then a loud and heartfelt, "Thank you, Lord Jesus, for forgiving me. I give my life to you now and forever." Wiping away the tears and smiling, he reached over, grabbed my hand, and profusely thanked me for my help. He said he felt reborn and full of hope, where there had only been hopelessness.

I mumbled something incoherent and said he was welcome. He rose, saying a ton had been lifted off his shoulders and assuring both Barbara and me that he would make the proper amends to his wife, family, friends and business associates. He then said goodbye, extolling the greatness and love of God. As he left, humming and happy, Barbara and I looked at each other, wondering what had just happened. We both knew we had had nothing to do with what had just transpired. In retrospect, I can now say, "Oh, the riches and mercy of God!" But then it was all a mystery.

Chapter 12

RESETTLING IN THOMSON

Shortly after all this, the District Superintendent called and asked if I would like to serve as an approved supply pastor on a three-church circuit on the Mississippi River. As long as I continued in school toward my Bachelor of Divinity, they would ordain me to these local churches. This meant I could marry, bury, baptize and serve communion.

Barbara and I took a day off and drove across the state to Thomson, Illinois, with a population of around 500 and the largest of these three churches, to consider this offer. The parsonage was located there, modestly boasting three upstairs bedrooms, a kitchen, dining room, living room, plus a basement. We felt we could stretch out there. The parsonage was old but in fairly good repair. The second of the three churches was in a small town a few miles east of Thomson called Argo Fay. It had a population of about fifty. The third and last church was out in the middle of the country in a place called Hickory Grove. It sat on a hill like a picture postcard. The congregations in each ran about 150 in Thomson, twenty in Argo Fay, and about seventy in Hickory Grove. We moved as soon as the school year was over in Evanston.

When we arrived in Thomson, a large flood was still receding. The Mississippi was many miles wide, at some places as much as fifteen miles. As we moved in, Barb, Becky and I met our neighbors. Two houses away was a family with a young boy of about ten who had spina bifida. He came down in his wheelchair to visit us. I took him upstairs to see the whole house since he had never been inside and was quite curious. Right next door to us on the north side was an old lady whose grandson had Down's Syndrome.

We later met her son and daughter-in-law who lived on a farm several miles from Thomson. She was a fine musician, and we enjoyed many wonderful evenings in their home. Just to the south of our house lived Joe, the Mayor of Thomson. He was a lineman, by trade, and had a lovely home. So it was that we settled in Thomson and a totally new life began for us.

After a few days I walked to the one block long main street of town. There was a gas station, a general store, a bank, and a small restaurant with two pool tables in the back. This was where the local district schoolboys congregated every day after school as well as evenings and weekends.

Having spent my growing-up years in a pool hall in Rockford, I decided to shoot some pool. I was all alone racking up for a game when the after school crowd came in. Seeing their disappointment that their table was being used, I told them to go ahead and I would watch. I watched for half hour or so when one of the boys, who had beaten everyone quite badly, asked if I would like to play him.

I said, "Sure," and he racked them up. I told him my name was Tom and my family and I had just moved to town. I broke the rack and none went in so he ran about three balls. I then ran about three, leaving nine balls on the table. The game was played to fifty balls so you had to play "position," concerning succeeding racks. He put two balls in, leaving seven; and I ran the next six, leaving the last ball in a great place for the next break. He and his friends seemed quite surprised and they all began rooting for him.

Without being too proud, I soon had beaten him by at least thirty balls. We had been playing for "time" so I thanked him and told him I would love to play again sometime. As I was leaving, he asked where I worked. He assumed I worked at the Army ammunition plant up by Savannah. When I told him that I was the new Methodist pastor and I hoped to see him in church on Sunday, the room went eerily quiet. I later found out I had made quite an impression on the town pool champ.

In fact, several of the boys who were around that pool table started coming to church. With them and others, we formed a youth group that ending up leading many other young people to the Lord.

Chapter 13

FROM SELMA TO SALVATION, THE REST OF THE STORY

As LATE SPRING turned into summer and the flood receded, Barbara and I prepared for the coming of our second child. This was further complicated as our marriage was in jeopardy. There was something going on in me that I was becoming more and more aware of. I was becoming increasingly morose and depressed. Thoughts of suicide plagued me daily as the only solution I could see for me and for my family.

These thoughts had occurred to me periodically but my Selma experience had pushed them to the fore. Politically, economically, and religiously, my life was in turmoil. Now with a marriage that was barely tolerable, these thoughts plagued me more than ever. I had waves of despair and hopelessness, coupled with overwhelming guilt.

My mind swirled with experiences that I had had with Edna Hutchins and E. Stanley Jones, as well as the book, *The Cross and the Switchblade* by David Wilkerson. And then there was Selma! I no longer had any basis to explain the meaning of life. I finally came to the place where I saw no way out of what to me was a living hell. Added to that was the responsibility of trying to pastor three little churches. I was a phony, through and through. How long would it be before the whole world knew it?

It was just before the birth of our second child, Paul, that I concocted a plan. I would drive my car into a railroad abutment I knew of not far from where we lived. The insurance would help Barbara and the family and they would be better off without me. Where do such dysfunctional, harmful thoughts come from? In retrospect, I believe suicide arises from a well-placed lie, one that the enemy plants in our minds as the only option to a dilemma. My plan was to go to my hometown of Rockford, sixty or so miles away and visit my old friend Paul Waters. He had been the choir director in my home church all through junior and senior high. Even though I had been away in the Army, we had maintained a wonderful friendship. My plan was to tell Barbara what I was going to do and then hit the abutment on the way there.

A few days later I said, "Goodbye," to my pregnant wife and headed for Rockford, determined that it would be the last ride I ever took.

The morning was gray and overcast. The traffic was light except for farmers on their way to feeding stock and milking their cows. I thought about my plan, as the abutment was about half way to Rockford. I felt I was thinking clearly, and I drove with a measure of peace. Soon I knew the abutment was around a couple of curves and then there would be at least three-quarters of a mile for a good straight shot into the railroad bridge. I could accelerate and reach a maximum speed and it would all be over very quickly.

As I rounded a bend, I saw the bridge. I said what I thought was a gallant, sacrificial prayer and put the pedal to the metal. As my speed quickly increased I felt a sense of destiny. This would be a helpful thing to do was the lie I told myself. Barbara and I were at the end of our marriage. The coming baby would never know me so there would be no loss. My insurance, although minimal, would enable Barbara to support herself and the children and also be enough for her to return to school. I knew both sets of in-laws would be there to help. I was further convinced that the churches wouldn't suffer, as they really didn't know me that well.

I was now about a quarter of a mile from the bridge. I could clearly see the abutment. I braced myself. The next few moments remain blurry to this day. I remember somehow careening away from the bridge, going through the "S" turn under the bridge, and almost rolling the car. I could hear and smell burning rubber. I fought the wheel to maintain control and, seemingly in a flash, was on the other side of the bridge. I pulled over onto the shoulder. I then shut the engine off and listened to the pounding of my heart. How long I sat there is a mystery. I sat there, feeling like a failure and a coward. I couldn't do anything right. I was a wimp who didn't deserve to live; I couldn't even kill myself properly. Eventually I started the engine. Telling myself I could kill myself later, I drove away. I decided that the way home would give me all the opportunity I needed and I would find the courage to do it then.

As I drove on toward Rockford, a deep anger and fear rose from within, a feeling of having been lied to about God—if there really was a God. I determined to get together with Paul and grill him about all of this phony God stuff. I arrived in Rockford about 10:00 a.m. and drove straight to Court Street Methodist Church, parking across the street. I walked through the huge front door and into Paul's choir office. I knocked on his door. We greeted each other warmly as he informed me it was his coffee break time and invited me to join him. I quickly agreed, asking if he had a little time to talk. He assured me he did, and off we went.

Exiting the church into the alley, we jay-walked across the street to a coffee shop that had been there as long as I could remember. We sat down and both quickly lit cigarettes. Ordering coffee, we soon got past the typical social pleasantries. I then launched into a tirade that even I hadn't anticipated. I wasn't loud or rude, but I was fiercely intense. I went into a long rant against the phoniness of the Church, in general, and of God, in particular. I vented my anger that we had been conned into believing there really was a God who gave a damn about anything. I let it be clearly known that, if I were God, I sure wouldn't let all of this crap in the world go on. If I had the power, I would stop wars and hatred. I would eliminate poverty. There would be peace.

I used my recent Selma experience and its aftermath as proof of an impotent God. In reality, there was no proof of God. I paused only long enough to light another cigarette, get more coffee, and prepared to blast him again. Paul said nothing. It seemed strangely comforting to me that there were no answers and even he knew it.

I had known Paul since junior high. He had gone through many of my teen experiences with me. Paul had been there the night I went through the windshield. He knew about my army years, the jobs I had had and both the good and bad decisions I had made. He watched me grow up, get married and start down my ministerial career path. Wisely he just sat there and let me blow it all out.

Over more coffee, I resumed my tirade. After a long while, I began to settle down. I recall having made really good points. I knew that Paul would have to agree with me. When I had finished, there was a long quiet pause. Taking another long drink of his coffee, Paul looked straight at me and said, "Tom, have you ever been born again?"

Before I could think, I replied, "C'mon, Paul, you don't really believe in all that simplistic, sentimental, emotional crap do you?"

He paused and looked down. His reply was, "You've tried everything else; it can't hurt and it might help." Then he asked if I had a better plan. I sarcastically asked if he meant praying some kind of Billy Graham prayer. He said that was as good as any and again, suggested I should try it.

I wanted very much to prove him wrong, so I asked him how to do that. He told me to pray something like this, "God, if you're real and knowable, and if Jesus really is your Son, and if there are answers to life, would you please show me the truth?"

Incredulously, I looked at Paul and realized he wasn't kidding. I thought, O.K. why not? I then said something similar to what Paul had said, adding a perfunctory Amen. There! I had done it, and nothing was happening. There were a few uncomfortable moments. Then we got up, Paul paid the bill, and we walked back to the church and said our goodbyes. I have a memory of kind of laughing to myself as though I had somehow won.

I left the church and headed back toward Thomson. I began to think that now truly was the time to eliminate myself, to do the right and manly thing. I tried to think about the bridge again, but I just couldn't seem to keep my mind on it. Instead, I saw how blue the sky was, how green the grass was, how cool, fresh and sweet the air smelled.

Suddenly, for no particular reason, I began to feel tears running down my cheeks. They were followed by weeping from somewhere deep inside me. Blinded by the tears, I pulled onto the shoulder and simply let my emotions go. I sat there in the car crying and sobbing. The strangest thing was that I wasn't crying out of sadness, but a joy I had only heard about. As I sat there recalling some of my past experiences, life seemed to begin to make sense. I cried, then laughed, then cried, then laughed until I was all cried and laughed out.

How long I sat alongside the road is still a mystery. Eventually I regained some composure, wiped my face dry, and found myself back on the highway. No sooner had I resumed driving than I began to sing, louder and louder. I was singing a solo I had sung as a young boy in the Wesley Boy's Choir. When I was in the Army, serving in the Philippines, my buddies always said that I was a "sweet drunk." I would get drunk and then sing all of this religious stuff, especially one song.

That was the song I sang that day in the car. The words came from a psalm, "*Oh, that I knew where I might find Him! Oh, that I knew where I might find Him, that I might come even to His feet, that I might come even to His feet. Oh, that I knew! Oh, that I knew! Oh, that I knew where I might find Him! I sink in deep mire where there is no standing, I am come into deep waters and the floods overflow me. Oh, that I knew! Oh, that I knew where I might find Him!"*

Even when I had been drunk, I had sung this over and over. Now, once again, I sang and sang these same, familiar words. Then I realized it! I had sung my way past the bridge abutment. I also I realized the presence I was experiencing had a note of familiarity about it. Many years later I would speak of it in this way, I hadn't found God, He had found me.

As I headed back to Thomson, past the bridge, I had the deep sense that everything was going to be all right: our marriage, family, ministry and whatever might lay ahead. I was filled with confidence. This confidence was in me and yet, strangely, was working without me! I now knew there was a God, not distant and uninterested in my life but, vitally concerned and aware of everything that had been going on.

One of my first revelations about this God was his humility. He hadn't seemed to demand anything of me. His only desire was to love, bless, and heal my life. I began to understand a little of what a minister named E. Stanley Jones had said many months earlier, "If God is like Jesus, I want to know and follow Him." Arriving back at the parsonage, I sat in the car and wondered what I was going to say to Barbara. I was becoming increasingly aware of a love for her that simply overwhelmed me. I wondered how I could have wanted to divorce her. I thought about our coming baby, now knowing that this new addition would be wonderful.

Chapter 14

THE VOICE IN THE BELLY

OVER THE NEXT several days I began to recall many of
the puzzle pieces of my life. These included an article by an
Episcopal priest about "glossalalia" or "speaking in tongues"
that had appeared in Colliers Magazine; the book *"The Cross
and the Switchblade,"* by David Wilkerson; the events
surrounding meeting Edna Hutchins, a godly woman who
had drawn me toward a Lord I didn't yet know; my meeting
the well known missionary to India, statesman and writer, E.
Stanley Jones; my work at the Board of Lay Activities and
the friendships I had made there; Selma, Alabama; the march
with Martin Luther King; the open-housing meeting; the
1964 election; my schooling as a young boy in Rockford; our
moving; the three churches; and finally my meeting with Paul
Waters.

Then there was the revelation Barbara had one morning
when a pastor in our District stopped by soon after my trip to
Rockford to greet us. As I talked to him that morning about
my experience, he remarked that it sounded like I had been
born again. Just then, Barbara walked out of the kitchen and
said, "What a quaint way of saying it; that's just the way I've
felt since last night. I've been born again! Yep! That's a real
neat way of saying it." Here is how Barbara recounts her
experience.

"My life as a young person was characterized by the ability
to make life altering choices with abandon. What made me
capable of living that way? Was it that I believed there would
always be a way out? Was it a foolish optimism or an immature
sense in invulnerability? Whatever it was, God knew all about

it. He used it to bring me to a face-to-face meeting with Him. There's no escaping a pre-existent, all-knowing, all-seeing, ever-present Creator God.

As I reflect on the early days of my marriage to Tom, I look back with eyes more familiar with the way God does things than the adolescent eyes of a disillusioned young wife and mother. I was vaguely aware that Tom and I were on a trajectory launched by an invisible, inscrutable presence lurking in the shadows of our life together. Any forward movement had been squeezing us both toward an apparent lose-lose decision. We could stay married and be miserable and frustrated; or we could divorce, go our own ways, and live with those unknown consequences.

Our situation was reflected in this experience we had recently: Tom and I were at an intersection waiting to make a left turn onto a busy thoroughfare. The driver in front of us wasn't signaling which way he was going to turn. "You jerk! Give us a clue, please…," I was thinking. He missed several opportunities to turn right or left leaving us both losing patience. At last he moved…straight through the intersection into a church parking lot across the street. My Abba Father reminded me, "Poor choices between two complete opposites are a strategy of the enemy. Don't forget, there is always a third option."

While Tom was calculating his way out of our dismal marriage, I was too. My heart's desire was to pursue an acting career in Hollywood or New York, but I was pregnant with our second child. My embryonic escape plan would have to be on hold for a while…meanwhile I began planning an exit strategy. However, there was a slight hitch… what if God were real? Now that would really mess up my hypothetical future!

As I lay in bed trying to sleep, I began weighing the consequences of my choices more realistically. A third option began to come into focus. If God were not real, then I was on my own; dependent on my wits, looks, connections, and talent to make my way in this world. Why go on with this Christian charade any further. On the other hand, if God were real and like the Jesus of the Scriptures, choosing to ignore Him would have eternal consequences. If I didn't chose to submit to this God, I'd be on the wrong side of life and truth. The loss would be incalculable.

I remembered the story of Rahab and her decision to side with the winners in the battle for Jericho. Then there was the parable Jesus tells about a King counting the cost before going to war (Luke 14:31-33). So, I lay there counting the cost. I reasoned, motivated by pure self-interest. If God is real, and He is truly God, then He can change my heart to embrace my husband and my children. He will have to take over my life.

I would have to live life the way He commanded, but He'd have to give me all I needed to do it. Surely to qualify as God of the universe, He would have the power to change my desires. If He was not real, I would know it soon enough. At least, I had to explore the possibility of his existence. So I did. There, lying in my bed next to my husband, I handed over control of my life and my future to an invisible Spirit Being. If He didn't accept me, I would be left to fend for myself. The deal was struck, and I fell asleep.

The awareness of a presence hovering near me awakened me. A living energy was dancing around and in me, not threatening, but welcoming. I knew this energy was the Spirit of God. His Holy Spirit assured me at a level deeper than thought that Jesus Christ was truly the Son of God and that He and His Father were in this Spirit accepting me into the family. I lay there absorbing the presence as if it were mother's milk. There was no doubt, I was home. I fell back asleep knowing that, over time; He would lead me through the demolition and reconstruction of my life to conform to His original design. With serene sleep, the adventure had begun."

Barbara and I had a long way to go but hope for the future was alive and blooming. We admitted to each other that we both had thought divorce was the only solution to our problems. We had never spoken to one another about it, afraid to broach the subject. We were amazed we had both been thinking the same thing. Now everything had changed. After the pastor left that morning, Barb and I wanted to read the Bible. We had never read it together and had only on very rare occasions prayed together. We started with John's Gospel. Each of us could only read a few verses until we would begin to cry at how beautiful it was, handing the Bible back and forth. Over the next months we read the entire New Testament out loud to one another with the same thrilling joy. We couldn't get enough. We both wondered why we had never enjoyed the Bible before. I had to study it for school but now it wasn't a chore but, rather, a delight.

I registered at a Lutheran School, Augustana, in The Quad Cities, majoring in Psychology. It was about this time I drove to Wheaton to meet Father Richard Winkler, the Episcopal priest I had read about in the Colliers' Magazine article. I was warmly greeted by his secretary and shown into a small chapel. I was filled with questions and he very patiently answered them all. Two hours later I asked him to pray for me to receive the Holy Spirit. He said that Jesus was the baptizer and all I had to do was ask Him to baptize me in the Holy Spirit. I did, and He did.

I instantly knew I had already received the Holy Spirit on my way from Rockford to Thomson that day after having been with Paul. There was a re-kindling of the joy of an inward river that I was now beginning to understand. Thanks to Father Winkler, I once again began to laugh, cry, and praise God; but he suggested that I cease praying and praising God in English and just begin to speak whatever "other language" the Holy Spirit might be giving me. Father Winkler didn't insist or demand anything of me; he just encouraged me to see what God might do. I stopped speaking in English, set my heart to praising God, and out of my mouth came this clear language. I first wondered if someone else had entered the small chapel; but, as I looked around, there were just the two of us. Father Winkler said I could pray in the Spirit anytime I wished, so for many minutes I started and stopped and it didn't go away. The language was always there. We said our goodbyes and I headed home, singing and praying in the Spirit almost all the way. After arriving at home and telling Barbara, she was very excited about having a similar experience.

Over the next few months, every Thursday Barb and I would drive about three hours for an evening prayer meeting in Wheaton. There were usually about twenty to thirty people. Those meetings were food for our spirits and we were so grateful for the practical working out of Life in the Holy Spirit that we experienced with these believers.

Also around this time the pastor, who had come to welcome us to the district, heard of the experiences I was having. He told us of a weekly prayer meeting at his parsonage in Lanark, just a few miles from us, where the gifts of the Holy Spirit were being manifested. This meeting was also held on Thursday nights so, after a couple more trips to Wheaton, we decided to travel to Lanark. Those meetings proved just as helpful and as full of blessing and revelation.

As the headquarters of my district of The Rock River Methodist Conference were in my hometown, I thought I should go and apprise the District Superintendent of my recent experiences. With a carefree heart I drove to Rockford to meet with the Superintendent. He graciously received me and asked what might be on my mind. I could hardly wait for him to hear everything. I excitedly babbled on for about forty-five minutes. After a long pause, he slowly said that he had heard of this type of thing happening and that I should be very careful not to be drawn into something that was peripheral, if not cultic. I later painfully learned that many, if not most, theological colleges and seminaries, whether Evangelical or Liberal, agreed at least on this one point of theology; the experience I had was done away with when the church received the scriptures.

This theology is called Cessationism. The principle is that with the death of the apostles, miracles ceased and the gifts of the Holy Spirit, given to start the church, were not needed after the church was founded. Then, much later in the 4th century, church leaders gathered together the sixty-six books of the Canon. Since then the Bible was to be our infallible guide in all things pertaining to life.

The upshot of my visit with the district superintendent was that he would talk with the pastoral relations committee and instruct them on how to deal with me. Thankfully, this wouldn't be for several months because he was quite busy. He also told me that I needed to be present at all pastoral district meetings. He admonished me that I was on dangerous footing in the conference. This, from a man who had previously said that he thought I had a bright theological mind with a bright future, left me in despair. I wondered if I might truly have been deceived. After all, he was a Doctor of Theology, my immediate superior, and had been a pastor for over twenty-five years before being appointed as District Superintendant.

As I drove over that same section of road where I had truly experienced the Lord for the first time just a few months before, my life was turned upside down again. Hope had burst in my heart. Once again I was thinking maybe I had been right all along; there really was no hope except in the power of man. I pondered this for a few minutes before deciding to ask Jesus about what had happened. I asked him if I was being deceived and if what I was going through was nothing more than a cultic experience. Immediately upon praying, my belly began to fill up as though it was about to explode. Without even thinking, I began to sing and praise God in language after language and was filled with joy.

I sensed a voice speaking from my belly, but resounding

in my head, "Son, do you desire to go back to where and what you had and the future that was then before you?" Instantly I said, "No, Lord, never!" I also sensed that voice saying that I must be aware that persecution was sure to come, and He would prepare me for it. I was not to fight, argue, debate, or defend myself in any way. I now belonged to Him and that was His business. I was barely out of Rockford city limits, but I felt loved, protected, and a lot more secure about what might lie ahead. I also knew that I had so much to learn. Arriving home, I told Barb everything. She was not at all threatened but absolutely excited, sharing in the same experiences that I was having.

Less than a week later the next pastoral district meeting took place in Savannah, Illinois, about twenty miles north of Thomson. I arrived at 8:45 for the morning meeting and soon most of the forty or so pastors had gathered. After the District Supervisor gave a word of prayer and the local pastor welcomed everyone, the meeting began. Time was taken up with lots of conference plans, the latest from Psychology Today, and what was, at that time, cutting edge theology: Situation Ethics, the God is Dead phenomenon, and Bultmann's demythologizing of the New Testament so that we could get back to the kernel of truth, what was called in Greek, the kerygma.

Most everyone seemed excited about this. However, I was not, and I felt a little out of place. After some lengthy discussion along these lines, the Superintendant asked if anyone had read some good books lately. I raised my hand, stating that I had just read a book that was of great help to me. It was *"World Aflame"* by Billy Graham. The silence was deafening. There were a few muffled comments, a long period of quiet, a few giggles, and then, after what seemed like a lifetime, the Superintendant said, "We must all forgive Tom as he is passing through a difficult time, having to come to grips with some bad theology; but I am hopeful he will come through it." I was embarrassed and humiliated. He then changed the subject and we broke for lunch.

When all had left the room, I sat there wanting to find a hole to crawl into. The District Supervisor stepped over to me, put his arm around my shoulder, and told me not to feel badly as we all have difficulties in life that we must surmount. I couldn't accept the idea that the experience I was having with Jesus was something I had to surmount. I could see that my days were numbered in that confession. I skipped the luncheon and headed home. When I told Barbara that I might no longer be a minister if what I sensed today were true, her response rescued me from self-pity. She said she had always enjoyed adventure, and now we were in an adventure with God!

Chapter 15

PREPARATION OF A SERVANT RATHER THAN A SERMON

THE NEXT FEW months of summer and fall in 1965 were filled with interesting events. On one particularly eventful day the Lord decided to talk to me about cigarettes, school and sermons. Regarding cigarettes, I had smoked at least a pack and a half of Pall Malls, Camels, Lucky Strikes, and Chesterfields daily since I was about 18. That day as I was driving down the road and enjoying a good smoke, the voice in my belly said, "Tom, you don't need those any more. Why not give them to me?" I responded out loud, "How?" The voice said, "Roll down the window and hand them out to me." I did, and He took them. As soon as that happened, my desire for cigarettes was gone—no withdrawals, just gone.

Then there was the issue of school. As I continued down the road, the voice said I was to drop out of school for now. This was frightening to me since I knew I needed a Bachelor's Degree to be fully ordained in the Methodist Church. Barbara and I had always agreed that we both must get our college education, at all cost. When I arrived home, I told Barb about dropping out of school. Her response was not nearly as strong as I had anticipated. Although I would have more college training in later years, to this day I have never received a degree. Barb and I have felt that God did not wish for me to rely in any way upon a pedigree of any kind. By no means did this mean that college or seminary was evil, but rather that I was not to go in that direction.

About fifteen minutes later the voice spoke again. "Tom, I want you to stop preparing sermons." Prior to this time I had taken at least twenty to thirty hours to prepare a sermon. I typed them out and read them verbatim. I usually began by thinking of some relevant thing that was a good and noble thought, then writing my sermon and, lastly, going through a concordance to find some scripture that vaguely related to my highest and best thoughts.

I had just been thinking about what I was going preach about on Sunday when the voice interrupted my thinking. I asked what I should say. As though avoiding my question the voice said, "I am going to prepare a preacher, no more sermons." The voice was deeply quiet and authoritative. I firmly said, "OK!" The following Sunday was going to be a brand new experience at the three little churches along the Mississippi River in northern Illinois that I had been assigned to.

Sunday morning arrived with my having tried to prepare something to say, but as hard as I tried nothing would come. I would think I had something but it seemed to vanish as quickly as it came. I awoke in a semi panic that Sunday morning, having absolutely no sermon. I left Barbara, asking her to pray, as I felt sure I was going to make a complete ass of myself.

The first church was Argo Fay. I usually got there about ten minutes before the 7:30 a.m. service, which lasted about forty-five minutes. A big crowd for Argo Fay was fifteen to twenty souls. We followed the order of service and after *The Hymn of Preparation,* it was time for the sermon. I stood up feeling paralyzed. I was preparing to tell them that I had no sermon when a thought came to me. It was that voice again. It was coming from my belly to my head, not originating in my own thoughts. "Tell them your story." I was about to answer, "What story?" when I realized where the Lord was taking me.

I told them about going to Rockford and seeing the music minister from my home church and what had happened as I gave my life to Christ. I was more amazed than anyone as my words began to flow, haltingly at first and then more easily. I ended by saying something like, "Isn't it wonderful that God is real and knowable?" We then sang *The Hymn of Invitation."* Amazingly enough, three people came forward, asking me to pray for them.

I had never given an "altar call" so this was entirely foreign to my experience. I just prayed, "Here are some people, Lord, and they want to be yours. Amen." I gave the benediction and walked to the rear of the church. Several of these sweet people rushed to thank me for the encouraging word. I jumped into my car and headed for the second church, Hickory Grove.

The service there ran from 8:30 A.M. until 9:30 A.M. giving me half an hour to make it back to Thomson for the 10:15 service. Argo Fay and Hickory Grove had Sunday school following their services and Thomson had theirs first, so it all seemed to work together. It was about a ten minute drive from Argo Fay back through the most gorgeous farmland you could imagine. Oh, how I loved the taste of cantaloupe, sweet corn, and other produce fresh from gardens, as well as beef and pork that melted in your mouth.

But there was no time to stop at a roadside stand that day. I arrived just as the service was about to begin. I hurriedly went to my seat behind the pulpit, next to the small choir loft. I began to wonder what was going to happen here. We followed the service outline and came to the same place. Right after *The Hymn of Preparation* I had a small but growing confidence that the voice truly would never leave me nor forsake me. I had begun to realize this voice was the gift of Jesus so that none of us would ever be alone again. It was the Holy Spirit. He, too, was a person and could be known and fellowshipped with. As unbelievable as it may seem, but blessedly true, He is just like Jesus. These thoughts were racing through my mind as I heard again, "Son, just tell your story." As I stood and looked out on these beautiful people, a love for them completely overwhelmed me. I scarcely could hold back my tears as I told my story about Jesus, His love, and forgiveness.

I was reminded of John Wesley's evening at Aldersgate, when he felt the love of God, that God was knowable and longing to have intimate relationship with us, and that He was not far away somewhere but closer than the things we could touch, feel, smell, hear, and see. Deeper than flesh and blood, He desired to live in our hearts, the deepest place within us, the real self, living by means of the uncreated, eternal life of God.

I suddenly was done speaking, with no further words from the voice. A seemingly uncomfortable silence followed and I just stood there not having a clue as to what to do. After about thirty long seconds, an idea came to me. I said that I had seen on TV, in one of Billy Graham's meetings, he had said it is a good idea to respond in some way to God's offer of relationship. So I suggested that anyone who would like to do so might walk from their pews up to the front, as a response. In retrospect, I think this must have been one of the clumsiest altar calls ever given because I didn't know what to do if anybody did come forward. I asked the organist to play something—anything—and I bowed my head and prayed, "Oh, God, help!"

Another thirty seconds went by, and then I heard shuffling. As I opened my eyes, I could hardly believe what was happening. Many people were wiping tears from their eyes, others were crying out loud, and still others had the most pleasant looks of joy on their faces. Several raised their hands, quietly praising and worshipping God. This was highly unusual. I had never in my life seen people in a Methodist church lift their hands, way up over their heads as though they were reaching for something, or Someone. I was transfixed as I watched about sixty of the seventy-five who were gathered that Sunday morning slowly make their way to the altar.

Some came and literally fell to their knees, others just stood before the altar weeping. Some stood quietly, tears streaming down their faces. Overwhelmed and speechless, I just sat down and cried, from a place inside me I would later learn was my new heart, a "real" new heart, and it was the real me! Several minutes later I sensed that something might need to be done. I asked if anyone had anything they would like to say. Several tried but could only joyfully cry.

There was another short pause and an old woman walked to the front. She said she had known all of them for years, most of them before they were born or married, and had also known their parents and grandparents. She had prayed that a time might come when the church she loved so much might once again be filled with the joy she had experienced all of her life. She had been lovingly apprehended by God as a little girl of eleven, and at times in recent years had wondered if that had just been something so personal and private that expecting others to have a similar experience would just make her critical, which she didn't want to be. This day her prayers, as well as her doubts and fears, were answered. She began to cry, softly at first, and then she burst into sobbing.

I was crying myself when one of the young men told me that I had better leave if I wanted to make it to my next service. I left, not having closed the service or given any kind of benediction. I walked to the car thinking whatever further needed to be done, God was well able to do. I pulled out of the parking lot and turned onto the gravel road that led to the main highway and Thomson. It would be about a twenty-minute drive and I prayed as best I knew how that whatever God wanted to do, I would not be an obstacle. As the town and the church building came into view, I sighed a last prayer of, "Help, God!"

Thomson was the largest of the three circuit churches. The usual attendance ran about ninety to one hundred. I saw Barbara walking down the sidewalk from our parsonage about a block away. I hurriedly stopped her and blurted out as quickly as I could what had happened. She laughed and, grabbing

Becky's hand, said she would see me after the service. I
made it to the chair up front, behind the lectern, just as the ten
voice choir began to sing the opening hymn. Perhaps eighty
five people were there counting the ten in the choir. It was a
beautiful day and everyone seemed in fine spirits.

The service followed the same liturgy and once again we
came to *The Hymn of Preparation*. As everyone was seated,
I waited for some kind of inner prompting. But nothing
immediately came. I stood there for an uncomfortable
minute or so, saying nothing. After about two minutes, the
congregation began to softly murmur. It was obvious that this
was a different Sunday morning than usual. I finally felt I
should read the Twenty-Third Psalm. I opened my RSV Bible
and began to read, "The Lord is my Shepherd I shall not want."

I abruptly stopped and began to speak about the meaning
of these words, asking questions about their meaning. Soon I
seemed to be in a stream of inner guidance that was prompting
me with bits of questions and information about this portion of
the first verse. I was saying things like, "What did the psalmist
mean when he said the Lord was his shepherd?" I further said
that I didn't really know what a shepherd was or did, and that,
if I did, I wasn't sure I even wanted a shepherd. The psalmist,
however, was telling us that his shepherd, whomever and
whatever he was, evidently filled his needs, resulting in the
statement that he had no wants! That would certainly be great if
it could be true for us also!

I went on to ask whether the scripture was really right
about this possibility, or was the Twenty Third Psalm just for
pretty needlework? Perhaps the psalm is just to create a sweet,
pastoral picture of nicer, more agricultural times when life
didn't seem to move as fast. Or could it be that The Living
God wanted us, in reality, to be as secure as a simple sheep
or lamb? By the time I got this far, I was talking faster and
more enlivened than I ever had before in my life. I must have
talked for at least twenty minutes before I realized I had gone

over the usual time of fifteen minutes. I had only gotten to the second verse, and I had so much more to say. However, seeing the clock at the back of the church, I stopped abruptly and apologized for going over time, assuring them that I would have more to say on this next week.

We sang the final hymn. I recessed down the aisle and gave the benediction from the rear of the church. As the people came out the door and I greeted them, I was blown away with the compliments, many saying they hadn't wanted me to stop. Others said they could hardly wait until next week. One I especially remember said that, for the first time, the Bible seemed to come alive. One after another they came out, even young children of six or so and especially the teenagers. Some wanted to know if I had thought about starting up a youth group. I said I didn't know, but I would sure think about it.

The last person out that Sunday was Marge. She was married to a farmer. I think they had three children, two older teen-age girls and a younger boy. She was so alive and gentle, and she sweetly encouraged me that this was exactly what the church needed.

As Marge locked up the church, I walked down the twelve or so concrete steps in front of the church, saying I'd see her later. I got in my car to drive the block or so home. When I got home Barbara immediately wanted to know where in the world I had gotten that sermon. I said I didn't know; it just sort of came out. She said it was great and hoped I would finish it

next week. I am blessed to say that the Lord has continued to lead me in this way over the years.

I must also say emphatically that through study of the Scriptures and the preparation I did, the

Lord created a hunger in me that was only satisfied by Himself, the true Bread of Life. This hunger was not for just Biblical or theological information but LIFE from the Tree of Life, Jesus Himself. I do not want to imply that the voice in the belly required nothing on my part. I am not passive or lazy in this process. The Lord asks of me that I lay down my life daily, and as I do, He does what only He can do. I think this is what Paul meant when he said: *"When I am weak I am strong."*

I have likened this to making percolator coffee. You put dry coffee in the basket and then add water. Soon the water boils and bubbles up and drips through the dry coffee grounds and voila, you have coffee. I would liken my part to supplying the dry grounds, ingredients like study, prayer, faith, and offering myself to the Lord. Then the Lord does his part, the boiling of the water, through the Holy Spirit's voice in the belly, and the provision of his resurrection Life. What comes forth is the true food of the Kingdom of God. I believe my part continues to grow over the years as I mature and humbly ask Him to conform me to the image of Himself.

Chapter 16

HEARING THE VOICE IN A SMALL TOWN

As Barbara and I began our new adventure in following God in the Spirit, the Lord began to use a variety of means to teach me how to hear His voice. Here is one of the early ones. Laverne and her daughter, Sally, lived in a little town in Illinois, one of the three churches that I covered on my pastoral circuit. They were both nurses and practiced in a small hospital in Milledgeville, not far from their home. One evening in the Fall of 1965 I received a telephone call that Laverne had been taken to Milledgeville hospital in great pain. I drove there within the hour and was told by Sally that X-rays had been taken of her mother's abdomen. She had both gallstones and kidney stones that were causing her abdomen to swell. Since no surgeon was available, they had called for one to come from Rockford. Her daughter told me they were just trying to keep her calm until emergency surgery could be performed. Sally gave me permission to see her mother but told me to be brief and to be as calm as possible. I agreed and walked down the hall to her room.

As I entered she was on the right-hand side of the room and had her hands clasped over her distended abdomen. She was grimacing and moaning with pain. To the left was a metal chair against the wall and a nightstand. Besides that, the room was bare. I sat in the chair a moment and then stepped across to her bedside. My thought was to pray quietly, blessing her and asking God's mercy and healing to be present. I also asked God to give me wisdom, thinking of James 1, which says when we are in need we should ask for help… and I was in deep need. As I stood beside the bed and began to pray, she opened her eyes and weakly acknowledged my presence.

Just as I was about to pray, the voice from deep within me said, "Ask her about her mother." I wondered what in the world was going on, so I overrode that voice with my mind and dismissed it. I began to pray again but immediately heard the same words. This time they came with greater intensity. "Ask her about her mother!"

I thought to myself that I might be hearing the voice of the enemy. I had come to believe there really was a malevolent spirit, known in scripture as the devil or Satan, and that the people in the Bible were not just "simpletons" who hadn't figured out how to deal with problems from a strictly psychological framework like in our culture. I fully believed that God had authored the scripture and there exists a very real enemy. So I made the decision in that hospital room to rebuke the enemy as if he was the source of the voice. Having done that, I started to pray a third time. I had barely opened my mouth when, again, I heard from deep within, "Tom, ask her about her mother!"

With all of my great discernment and authority, I began to think that perhaps I should obey the voice. I turned to Laverne and sweetly and very softly said, "Laverne, tell me about your mother." What happened next absolutely scared the hell out of me. She rolled over like a hog on a spit and, with eyes of intense hatred, verbally spit at me that her mother should be tortured and sent to burn in hell eternally. There was so much force in her words that I felt an invisible hand pushing me backwards into the metal chair across the room. I hit the chair with a thump, thinking, "Oh, my God, what have I done?" I was supposed to keep her calm; now she could explode and I would be guilty of killing her. She let out some more foul words about her mother I hadn't heard since my drill sergeant in the army had yelled at us. She then rolled over toward the wall and began to moan loudly.

Stunned, I sat in the chair, my heart pounding, scared to death. What in the world was wrong with me? It was my responsibility, as her pastor, to bring some prayerful comfort; but I had caused her more pain. I don't remember how long I sat there. I was shaking so badly that I was completely unaware of time. Finally, I regained some composure and, looking towards the door, hatched a plan. I would walk quietly to the bed, lay my hand very gently on her head, and bolt out the door, leaving the poor woman alone. I arose with much fear and little confidence and walked toward the bed. I held my hand out to touch her head. To my own great surprise, I said, "Laverne, tell me more about your mother."

I had just gotten the words out of my mouth when she exploded again, "Damn it! Didn't you hear me the first time? That woman should roast in hell!" Again there was a supernatural force in the room that pushed me back across the room into the same metal chair. I thumped down again and thought, "I must have the gift of stupid!" One thing I did notice, however, was that the second salvo only had about half the strength of the first. I was still scared, but after several moments of listening to her moan, I decided to quickly walk across the room and say, "Bless you, Laverne," and get out of the room. Summoning my shaking frame to its feet, I started to walk by and say, "Bless you," when I heard that voice again. This time it was so loud inside me I looked around the room to see if anyone else might have heard it. I opened my mouth and said, "Laverne, if you will forgive your mother, God will heal you!"

Again she rolled over quickly and started to speak, but this time without the intensity. She said, "Pastor, you wouldn't believe what that woman did to me." She began to pour out stories of abuse to a young girl that were beyond belief. The stories broke my heart. She recounted incident after incident for ten or fifteen minutes. As I listened, I began to get a clue! Perhaps this was God at work! When she finally stopped, she began to cry softly, saying she hadn't cried since she was a little girl and was a bit ashamed to be doing it in front of me. There were a few moments of intense quiet, and then the voice spoke again, "Ask her to forgive her mother."

So I said very softly to her, "Laverne, forgive your mother and God will heal you. He loves you so much and wants you well, but if you don't forgive your mother, this or other problems will just come back." She started to protest with a mixture of fear and hope in her eyes. She then began to cry, only this time it increased to deep, uncontrollable sobbing that went on for several minutes. As the sobbing slowly subsided, her eyes changed along with her demeanor; and, like a little girl, she timidly asked, "Do you really think God would do that?" Still shaken and confused, I finally realized that something divine was taking place here. I assured her He would, with a confidence far deeper than anything I had ever experienced. She smiled a little-girl smile and said, "OK, Pastor." She gripped my hand and prayed a simple prayer, "Mother, I forgive you," and then added, "God, would you please forgive me and wash away all the hatred and bitterness I passed on to my husband and daughter and others over the years. Amen." She then opened her eyes that were wet with tears and said, "Pastor, please pray for me." I asked her to lay her hands on her swollen abdomen and I placed mine over hers. I simply said, "Heal her."

I watched for the next five minutes as her abdomen, that had been grossly swollen, slowly returned to normal. Laverne's tears, along with mine now, turned to awe, wonder, and amazement. Her face began to glow with a heavenly joy and we just kept saying together, "Thank you, thank you!" over and over. Soon all the pain was gone and she wanted to get out of the bed. I urged her to stay still and told her I would get her daughter. She agreed and began to hum quietly as I left the room, not really sure what had just happened.

Opening the door into the hallway and heading for the nurses station, I must have had an Andy Griffith grin from ear to ear as I approached the nurse's station. Her daughter looked up at me with a shocked expression, wondering what I was so happy about. I told her she should come with me. She quickly came from behind the counter and, looking at me strangely, nearly ran to her mother's room. Upon entering, she saw her mother sitting up in bed with a big smile on her face. Sally was stunned and speechless, and then Laverne said, "I'm fine. God just healed me." Her daughter, looking from her mother to me said, "What did you say?" Laverne repeated, "God healed me." Sally began to cry, I began to cry, and the three of us just cried. Later I was told they took more X-rays and found all traces of gallstones and kidney stones gone. They dismissed her from the hospital the following morning.

Many years later, remembering such incidences, I ask myself why it seemed to take so long for me to learn to hear and obey the Lord's voice. Why in the past forty plus years have I been so easily thrown off the path of simply following Jesus? Perhaps that is why I'm writing some of my story down. Perhaps others can avoid some of my pitfalls and I can encourage other faltering souls to rise up and listen for the voice of their God. It will be well worth the effort if just one person is able to find their road in Him again. The whys of today resonate in my heart, not critically like a hammer of condemnation, but rather as the scars of an oft-wounded warrior who knows now, better than ever before, that we have a speaking Lord and that He can be trusted to lead. Let us be encouraged to follow on to know Him.

Following the Lord Brings Joy and Sorrow

Following the incident with Laverne I would soon encounter a situation that baffled me. In our fellowship, there was a family that had a fourteen-year-old girl, Linda, with leukemia, as well as her brother who was twelve, with spina bifida. After seeing what had happened with Laverne, I began to think perhaps the same thing could happen with this family. I want to emphasize something I did not know about God at

that time: every situation has its own reality and purpose in
God. This may sound heretical, perhaps there is another way
of saying it, but here is what I've come to after all these years:
DO NOT LIVE BY PRINCIPLE, BUT BY LIFE! That does
not mean God is without principle, but it does mean He is God.
As the Psalm says, "God sits in His heaven and does as He
pleases."

I had come to know the family fairly well as they attended
church regularly and were always ready to help others. Mrs.
McBride, the mother, always seemed to have a chronic sadness
about her, while her husband, Jack, was always on the edge of
tears and/or anger. I can only imagine the struggles they were
experiencing on a daily basis. I learned that church hadn't
been of much help in their finding comfort. They heard about
what happened to Laverne and began to think perhaps there
was some hope for them. They asked what they had done
wrong that they had two children who would not live very
long. Another question was, "Did God really care?" And then
the guilt would rise in them for somehow maligning God.
The guilt gave way to anger, yet the only thing the church
and its ministers had been able to say to them was that there
might soon be a cure. This was true enough, but it didn't help
their hurting hearts as they helplessly watched their children
slowly dying. They also bore the terrifying possibility of
bringing another child into the world with the same illnesses.
They had both wanted to have a large family. Jack was a great
outdoorsman and had looked forward to hunting, fishing and
camping with his children. Now he couldn't do any of that for
fear of infection for Linda, or discouragement for his son.

I recall the morning as being one of those known only to
people who live by a body of water. In this case, it was the
receding spring flood of the mighty Mississippi. A lazy fog
hung over the highway as I headed north to Savannah hospital.
I had gotten a call that a young couple in the church had just
had a baby and were ecstatic, after years of being unable to
conceive. The doctor's best guess was that their chances of

having children were slim to none. However, one steadfast older lady in the little church at Hickory Grove had suggested that the church pray for them and the woman did, indeed, conceive. Everyone felt this was an answer from God.

I drove the twenty or so miles to the hospital with a light heart looking forward to rejoicing with them. I arrived a little after 8 o'clock in the morning and went immediately to the maternity ward. I found the young mother in bed, nursing her newborn and waved at her and smiled, saying I would wait until she was done. I sat in the corridor outside and, as I waited, the husband came down the hall with a giant bouquet and a grin that lit up the hall. As we talked he went on and on about his miracle baby boy. He said he almost wanted to name him Jesus, but I was not to worry, he knew that wasn't a good idea. Soon I got a chance to see the beautiful little boy. Dick and I went in and he tenderly kissed and hugged his wife while at the same time looking for something to put the big bouquet into. We all must have sat there for five minutes, smiling, laughing and praising God. Shortly thereafter both sets of in-laws arrived and we re-rejoiced again. It was a joyful time.

About fifteen minutes later the floor nurse asked if I was Pastor Mohn. I said, "Yes," and she told me I was needed downstairs in the emergency room. I quickly said my goodbyes and took the elevator to the first floor. I hurried to the emergency room but it was empty except for the staff. I asked if anyone knew why I had been called and an orderly said that Jack was on his way to the hospital and that my wife had contacted the hospital, asking them to locate me. Just then Jack drove in the hospital driveway.

Stopping quickly and rushing to open the back door of the car, he tenderly picked up Linda and, half-running and half-walking, came toward us. I will never forget Jack's face, streaming with tears, yet talking as fast as he could as the orderlies rushed to meet him. Linda's frail, limp body hung like a rag doll in his arms. The orderlies took her quickly as the emergency-room doctor came running out. Putting her on a gurney, the doctor walking briskly alongside was already beginning to work on her. All the time Jack was saying he had done everything he knew to do, but she had stopped breathing. I embraced Jack and we followed them all into the hospital.

They asked Jack and me to stay in the waiting room. Jack didn't want to leave his daughter, but they told him they would let him know as soon as they knew anything. I hurried him into the waiting room where we asked for God's mercy. It seemed like forever. Thirty minutes later the doctor came out and sadly told Jack there had been nothing he could do to revive her and that she must have died on the way to the hospital. The doctor then put his arm over Jack's shoulder as I put mine over the other, and we walked into the room where her body lay. Jack rushed over, picking up and cradling her body in his arms, and wept and wept. The doctor and I could do no less, and we all stood together, weeping, for several minutes.

Soon, however, the doctor was called out of the little cubicle and Jack and I stayed there for a long time. Soon Jack's wife, Martha, arrived with their son and I told them Linda had died. Martha and Billy went into the emergency room and all of them cried together. I had gone into the cubicle for a short time with the family but had stepped out to give them some time alone. I sat down in the waiting room, alternately crying, thinking, and praying. In less than an hour I had gone from great joy over a miracle baby, to deep sadness over the death of a darling little girl of fourteen. As I thought about Jack, Martha, and Billy, I felt absolutely empty. What help could I be to them? Here I was, their pastor, and I had nothing to say to them, no words of comfort, no wisdom from God; all I could do was cry with them.

It was then that I very faintly heard the inner voice. The Lord was saying to me, "Tom, that's all you're supposed to do. Weep with them. This is too big for you and them. Now give it all to me." As I recall, this was the first time I ever heard the phrase I was to hear hundreds of times over the next decades, "Son, it is good to remember that I am God and you are man." There have been many variations on this theme over the years, but it has always been comforting.

The day that Linda died I went about making arrangements for her funeral. This was only the second funeral I had ever officiated. My only preparation was one class on how to counsel the sick and the dying, which, frankly, had been fairly meaningless. Trusting God to bring comfort to real people in real grief wasn't emphasized much at all. Part of my experience so far in the Methodist Church had caused seeds of cynicism toward the church and organized religion in general. It would take several years for that cynicism to finally be dealt with. I was grateful that at least now I had some experience with a living God, without which I could never have made it through the next few days. My cynicism was simple. All I felt I had received from the church were religious platitudes. It seemed to me that we adults were involved in this religious game that we were to pass on to our children. We all knew it was a bunch of nonsense, but the traditions were good for the culture, providing continuity and some familial stability. So, why not perpetuate the lie? This cynical attitude nearly pushed me over the emotional edge more than once.

Along with this critical attitude and cynicism were now the recent experiences with a living God that threw everything into emotional and mental disarray. What was happening? What was real? Within the last month I had tasted of some things I could not deny, and yet my heart and mind were swirling, trying to find some kind of solid foundation, a place to stand. Was there a place I could always go to and be certain? Was God that place? If so, was there a means, a way of getting to Him? What was I supposed to do? It was all so confusing, and I felt very small!

The funeral itself was a blur. I remember many people packing the church and a lot of kids from Linda's school. I wish I could say that I was able to offer something profound and helpful, not only to the family but to friends and relatives. The truth is that I mostly read scripture, interrupted often by tears, and I can recall saying nothing especially meaningful. At the graveside, I again read several scriptures and cried as they lowered her body into the ground. "Ashes to ashes and dust to dust, etc...." The people came and cried and hugged the family and then quietly moved away until they also turned and left the cemetery. I stood transfixed, unable to move as I watched them enter the funeral limousine. I stood there, my feet planted, as if desiring to grow into the soil and cried and cried as time stood still.

My solitude was broken by a voice that said, "Pastor, is something wrong? We need to fill the grave now." I was caught off guard and embarrassed, and probably said something innocuous as I walked away to my car. I closed the car door, my mind full of questions and accusations about God, life, and death. The "whys" were so loud I was certain even the gravediggers heard them. How long I sat in the car waiting for some semblance of emotional stability to take place is still fuzzy in my memory. Slowly, I came to myself, started the car, and headed for the wake. The wake also remains a blur, but I do recall arriving home later, drained and feeling very protective and possessive of Barbara and Becky. I wanted to hold them and never ever let them out of my sight.

Chapter 17

MIRACLES AT A CONVENTION AND TOUCHING THE SHEKINAH GLORY

A PASTOR FRIEND called and told me about a convention in St. Louis he thought I might enjoy and invited me to go with him. It was being held by the Full Gospel Businessmen's Association. I told him I had never heard of that group, but figured I needed a diversion. This was in the spring of 1966. In a few days we were on our way to the Chase Park Hotel in St. Louis. Except for one long, scary night at a Pentecostal church in South Chicago with a speaker named Derek Prince, I had never been around Pentecostals.

We arrived, registered, got settled in our room and went downstairs to eat. The lobby was bustling with dozens of men. I think the conference must have accommodated between 800 and 1,000. I was totally unprepared for the happenings of the next two days.

It all began when I walked through the lobby and a man, whom I did not know, called me, gaining my attention. Then, breaking free of his clique of friends, he came bolting across the room, aimed right at me. My friend seemed startled but assured me he knew this guy and he wasn't a nut. I later learned that his name was Dr. James Brown from Upper Octarara, in Pennsylvania. He was the pastor of the oldest Presbyterian Church in America. He was taller than me and grinningly accosting me, he said he had a message for me. I immediately thought he must be an employee of the hotel and there was some emergency back home.

I said, "What is it?" expecting a piece of paper or some

verbal direction to the front desk or nearest telephone. Instead, he looked me right in the eye and began telling me about my future, the call of God on my life, and much more. He abruptly finished and said, "That's it!" and he turned and walked away as abruptly as he had come. Before I could think, I turned to John and said, "What the hell was that?" John was laughing and said he thought we ought to find a quiet place for some dinner and he would try to explain, what the hell had just happened.

We snaked our way out of the lobby into the street and saw a small restaurant. Hurrying across the street, we soon found ourselves seated at a private table. John seemed to think this all very funny, but I was nonplussed, to say the least. After we ordered and the waitress left, John slowly began to educate me concerning the world of Pentecostalism. After John had become a Methodist pastor, he had some of the same experiences I recently had. The result for him had been explosive and, for the past year or two, he had been wondering what was going to happen to him in the Methodist Church. I learned later, after we had moved to Tulsa that things became uncomfortable and he and the District Superintendent agreed it was best for him to leave. I believe he did go on to pastor a Pentecostal church somewhere back east. I've not seen him since.

Anyhow, back to St. Louis and my education. He said that Pentecostals believed in what they called a second blessing. They called this the Baptism in the Holy Spirit. Their theology said that after a person is born again, or saved, there is another experience whereby that person is filled with the Holy Spirit and given the gift of speaking in unknown tongues as a sign of having been filled. Generally, if there are no tongues you haven't been filled and must wait until this happens.

Starting there, John walked me through the Old Testament regarding the promise of the Holy Spirit. After about forty-five minutes or so he came to the Corinthian letter where Paul talks about the gifts of the Holy Spirit. He said this is what had happened to me earlier that evening. Dr. Brown had felt led of the Holy Spirit to come and give me a prophetic word. I, in turn, was to either reject or accept it as a word from God. If it was from God, I was to act accordingly. John finally stopped and asked, "Well, brother, what do you think? Was it a word from God for you or not?" My response was, "How the hell do I know?" John laughed and said we would talk about that later. We paid our bill went back across the street and into my first Full Gospel Businessmen's meeting. I was in for a ride.

The first thing I noticed was that the worship was loud, happy, and physical, and it went on for at least an hour. The speaker that night was Oral Roberts. My only contact with him had been to mistakenly watch him as I switched channels on the television. So once in awhile I would catch a glimpse of him before I could change the channel, with the same cynicism, I might add, with which I had watched Billy Graham. I knew he believed in healing and that was about all I knew about him.

Demos Shakarian, the conference coordinator, then introduced him and said that Oral Roberts would be having weekend seminars at his fledgling university in Tulsa, OK. He encouraged any who wanted more information to come after that evening's meeting. With all of my cynicism, suspicion, and critical heart, I remember folding my arms and saying to myself, "O.K. Mr. Roberts, show me your stuff!" As he walked to the podium, the crowd rose to its feet, clapping and praising God. He finally had to quiet them down before he could begin. He opened his King James Bible, read a passage and then began to tell a portion of his story.

The story was about an Oklahoma boy with Cherokee Indian roots who wanted to be a basketball player and governor of the State of Oklahoma. When he was seventeen, while playing a basketball game, he collapsed, coughing and bleeding profusely from his mouth. The diagnosis was tuberculosis. This just about destroyed him, and he grew distraught and angry with God. He finally came to a point where his sister said that an evangelist was near by who prayed for the sick and she wanted him to go. She said, "Oral, God is going to heal you." Oral said that those words found root in his heart and, sure enough, he went, was prayed for, and was, indeed, healed. His whole life was turned around.

I noticed that during his talk he never spoke very loudly or was dramatic in any way. His language was simple, sincere, and to the point. He finished in about forty-five minutes and then directed anyone who would like prayer to come forward so he and others on the dais could pray for them. I noticed Dr. Brown was excitedly embracing Oral as people began to flock to the front. I watched for a long time and they prayed for every person who wanted prayer. Finally the meeting broke up with an announcement that Derek Prince would be the speaker at the morning breakfast. John wanted to stay for a while, but I was dead tired and went up to bed.

Morning came and I found myself at breakfast with a young Baptist pastor from Pascagoula, Alabama. He was delightful, and very funny. There were about eight at our table and one was saying that he would like to see a miracle personally to answer all of his doubts about healing and all this charismatic stuff. The morning meeting started with many testimonies. At about 10:00 o'clock Derek was introduced and spoke on healing in the atonement. He spoke in a clipped British accent and, like Oral Roberts, was neither dramatic nor emotional. He had been a Philosophy professor at Cambridge University in England before becoming a Christian. His talk was much more scholarly, very organized, and easy to follow; you could tell he had given many lectures.

He finished about 11:00 a.m. and again directed any who would like to be prayed for to come forward. The front filled quickly with people, and I was among them. The guy from our breakfast table who had said he needed to see a miracle was right next to me as people were being prayed for. Directly in front of us was a man with a white, blind-person's cane. We could see his eyes were covered over with some kind of white stuff. Having seen him around the meeting before, we knew him to be blind. As others were being prayed for, he came right up to Derek Prince. Derek asked what the man wanted. He said he wanted prayer for his eyes to be healed. Derek laid hands on the man, anointing his eyes with oil. This anointing thing was also new to me.

They prayed several seconds and the man threw the cane in the air and cried out, "I'm healed! I can see!!" As the crowd broke out in wild praise, the man turned right around in front of me and his eyes were as clear as could be. He pushed by me and began to run, all the while yelling, "I can see! I can see!" I stood there stunned, my mouth hanging open. I had seen his eyes before and now—Wow! I felt as if I was back in the time of Jesus and part of the crowd which followed him. I turned to my breakfast companion and said, "Did you see that? We saw him before, the guy's healed!" The guy who had wanted to see a miracle turned to me and said, "This is a crock! How stupid do they think we are?" He angrily turned around and, before I could say anything more, strode through the crowd and out the back door. I never saw him again. John, who had not been near the incident, later asked if I had heard about the blind man being healed and I reported to him all I had seen.

Many other things happened that weekend that defy explanation. Several things, however, remain clear in my mind. Firstly, these people believed in a God who truly was omnipotent, omnipresent, and omniscient. The difference was that this was not a theology but a living reality. Secondly, there was always the expectancy and opportunity for God to do something. The meetings were always subject to change. Thirdly, there seemed to be genuine love for people. Lastly, there was a generosity I had never seen. As John and I drove home, we were both aware that nothing was ever going to be the same again. God was real and present. Barbara and I had better put on our spiritual seatbelts because we were in for a ride.

The Shekinah Glory

Just south of Thomson was an old town named Fulton just across the river from Clinton, Iowa. We shopped in Clinton at least once a week, and it was on one of those trips I heard of a morning prayer meeting in Fulton, sponsored by a group of ministers. The meeting was a "get-to-know-each-other" meeting, sponsored primarily by the Reformed community. I made a note and at 6:00 a.m. the following Monday I drove to the Reformed Church where I met five pastors: one Pentecostal, three Reformed, and one Presbyterian. The following week at this prayer meeting I met Father Bill, who at 6' 8" tall was one of the tallest men I knew and who was also very personable. Together, Father Bill and I were to experience one of the most awesome encounters of either of our lives.

After a month of my attending these meetings, we agreed to go across the river to Clinton each Monday after our prayer time for a swim at the local Y.M.C.A. This turned into a really fun time. On one such occasion, I mentioned to the group that Billy Graham was going to be on television that week and invited anyone who would like to come up to our parsonage in Thomson to have dinner with us and then watch it. The only taker I got was Father Bill.

The following Thursday night he arrived at 6 o'clock for dinner. After dinner we played with Becky for a while and then as the 8 o'clock program approached, Barbara, now very pregnant, decided to put Becky to bed and go to bed herself. She did come down, however, after Becky was asleep, and watched the remainder of the broadcast with us. After it was over, the three of us began to pray. After about half an hour of excited prayer, Barbara decided it might be a long night and went upstairs to bed. I had told Bill about my experiences with the Holy Spirit, i.e. praying in tongues, healing, etc. and my having come to believe that these gifts were still available to Christians today. Father Bill showed great interest and wondered if he could experience this also. During his studies for his pontifical doctorate, the subject had been broached but never followed through.

That night, as we began to pray together, he asked if I would pray with him to receive the baptism in the Holy Spirit. I said I would and prayed quite simply, "Lord Jesus, you are the One who baptizes in the Holy Spirit. Would you please pour out your Spirit upon Bill." After praying this, I began to sing "in the spirit." As I did, Bill wanted to know where I had learned that song. I said I didn't know; the Holy Spirit was giving it to me right then. I assumed I was worshipping in the spirit and had given no thought as to what I was singing. It sounded like a simple children's song in a language totally unfamiliar to me. As I continued to sing it over and over several times, he asked me where I had learned Gaelic. I said I didn't know Gaelic and asked what that was. He said it was the original Irish language and that I was singing a lullaby his mother had sung to him as a little child when putting him to bed. I was singing it in perfect Gaelic. He and I were both stunned, but soon the song stopped and I continued to speak in Gaelic. This time it was a message to Bill from God, calling him to a deeper walk in God. Bill was thunderstruck, as was I.

Then, without warning, the whole room brightened up. About that time Bill fell off the couch onto the floor into a joyful, sobbing ecstasy of praise and thanksgiving to God and he began to speak in tongues. Louder and louder, we both prayed and sang for perhaps thirty minutes. I had been sitting on the couch while Bill was face down on the floor. During most of this time my eyes had been closed. I had noticed earlier, however, that the room seemed brighter than usual. Then, as I opened my eyes, I became aware of something strange. I looked all over the room and there were no shadows. I got down off the couch and crawled along the floor, trying to find out what was so different. As I did, I asked Bill to open his eyes and tell me what he thought was going on. He could barely lift his head off the carpet, but opening his eyes, he cried out, "Oh, my God, Shekinah!"

I said "Shikki what?" Bill looked up, this time in tears of

joy and wonder, and again yelled, "Oh, my God! Shekinah!"
He couldn't hold his head up for very long and I said again,
"What's a Shek-whatever?" This time I began to intensely look
around the room. There were no shadows anywhere; I mean
anywhere--none under the chairs, behind the couch, under the
tables--it was all light. I couldn't even make a shadow with
my hand against the wall the light of the lamp. Unbelievably,
there were no shadows anywhere. I finally began to realize
that something was going on that was very, very unusual. As
I crawled around the room, looking under, over, and around
everything, I looked into the dining room and could see that it
was dark.

After a few minutes, Bill stopped sobbing and began to
laugh. Slowly pulling himself up to a sitting position, wiping
his eyes, and cleaning his glasses, he told me what Shekinah
was. In the Old Testament, after Solomon had finished building
the temple and was dedicating it, the Glory of God filled the
temple and the priests couldn't stand up to minister, they were
laid out on the floor. The dedicated temple was filled with light.
This is what Bill was trying to tell me, but he couldn't speak.
He also said he had felt a heavy hand on his back while he was
lying on the floor, and he could not move.

As Bill finally got up off the floor and we both sat back on
the couch, the light slowly faded away. It probably took about
five minutes for normalcy to return to the room. After drinking
some more coffee and singing and praising and wondering
about all that had just happened, Bill felt it was time to go
home and be alone with the Lord. Even though it was after
midnight when Bill left, I stayed up about half an hour longer
before going to bed, feeling a little like the shepherds must
have felt on the night Jesus was born when the angels had
appeared.....and they wondered. I also "wondered" for many
days, as I still do, why God had been so gracious to Bill and
me. He must have known that I needed a kind of a jump start to
my Christian faith.

Chapter 18

ORU YEARS

As we continued in Thomson, our hunger for God was growing. At the same time I was growing more dissatisfied with my theological education. I had taken some courses at Augustana College and a seminar course at Dubuque Seminary on Dietrich Bonhoeffer. I was disappointed in them, however, as there seemed so little passion for truth, yet an agenda for revisionism. After reading the three required books on Bonhoeffer, I felt as though I had read completely different books than my professor was discussing. He made Bonheoffer sound like a Universalist or a Deist, with little allegiance to the person of Jesus Christ. He presented a view that made Bonheoffer appear to be suspect of scripture as a basis for faith and truth. To be "born again" was ridiculed quite openly, disdaining such an experience as a sign of intellectual deficiency. Christianity, from his point of view, was outmoded. I had run into this same view at North Park College in Chicago.

Evangelicals were openly mocked as those who couldn't think for themselves, were naïve and simple-minded. It seemed the only acceptable viewpoints were extremely liberal. Psychological truth reigned supreme. As a result of Bultmanns' demythologizing of the scriptures, the miracles of Jesus were all suspect. Liberal professors were beginning to vote on the actions and sayings of Jesus, later codified in *The Jesus Seminar.* The professors, mostly Ivy League scholars, would go through the New Testament voting on various passages. They used red beads to indicate things they were sure Jesus said or did, pink beads to indicate things Jesus probably did, gray beads to indicate the passage was not said by Jesus but contained his thoughts, and black beads to indicate Jesus did not do what was written there. To me this was the height of arrogance. Millions of denominational dollars were being funneled into every liberal cause. I would later understand, although not necessarily agree with, the Southern Baptist backlash of Colleges and Seminaries against these teachings. Relativism reigned supreme and any suggestion that there were absolutes was cavalierly dismissed. This is the educational and theological climate into which I was "born again."

Thus it was that I felt very excited when a friend suggested I go to Tulsa, Oklahoma, to a new university and seminary being started under the auspices of Oral Roberts. It would be called Oral Roberts University. Barbara and I were invited to a weekend at ORU. That, indeed, was a weekend to remember. We were met at the Tulsa Airport and driven to the new campus, where we were warmly greeted and escorted to our dorm room. While going up an elevator to our first meeting we met Tommy Tyson. Little could I imagine the impact he would have on my life. He was the first campus pastor/chaplain at ORU and was a Methodist, so I felt comfortable with him. While going up the elevator that day, a young student was holding her cheek in obvious pain. She had just had some dental work done and was going to lie down. Tommy asked her about the pain and then gently laid his hand on her cheek and prayed for her as we went up. It was a short, sincere, and obviously appreciated prayer. By the time we reached the fourth floor, the disembarking the girl smiled and said that his prayer was a real help.

The first thing I observed on the campus was all of the spontaneous prayer and seeming joy. People were open, congenial, and truly concerned that our stay be an enjoyable one. We went to the first meeting where I was taken aback with the worship and praise that seemed to go on and on. After thirty minutes of worship, Ron Smith welcomed us to the ministers' seminar and introduced those who would be speaking, Oral Roberts, Tommy Tyson, Dr. Howard Ervin, and an evangelist named Velmer Gardner.

Velmer proved to be a delight; as an old-time evangelist he told of preaching on the Red Sea parting for Moses. After his message, a modernist, as Velmer called him, came up and said he could easily destroy his whole message. Velmer asked how and the man preceded to tell him that a scribal error had mistranslated the verse about the Red Sea and that is was really the Reed Sea which only contained at the most a foot of water. Velmer surprised the man by yelling and rejoicing and praising God. The man asked why he was so happy. Velmer replied that if what he had just told him was true that it was an even bigger miracle than the Bible recorded. The man said "How so?" Velmer replied that, if that were true, Pharaoh and his whole army had drowned in 12 inches of water!

That first evening turned out to be a little much for Barbara and me. After the meeting, which included loud praise, worship in tongues, messages in tongues, and even some prophecy and dancing, we were overwhelmed and wanted to go home. We called a cab and asked the driver to take us to the nearest restaurant and bar. We found out that alcohol was not sold openly in Oklahoma. He knew, however, a place where we could find a drink. We had a beer, a bite to eat and some wine, and talked until one or two in the morning, wondering what in the world we might be getting ourselves into. Was this a giant cult? Were we deceived? Was our District Superintendent right about all of this stuff just being emotional hype? Had we been hoodwinked by our naiveté? We found our way back to our dorm room, avoiding people for fear they would cast demons out of us if they smelled alcohol on our breath.

We rose fairly early in the morning, had breakfast, and wandered into the morning meeting. This was the first time that I heard Tommy Tyson speaking and my interest was piqued. He spoke simply, telling his own story of being one of five brothers, all of who were Methodist preachers in the North Carolina and Virginia Conferences. He graduated from Duke Seminary, having been taught some of the same theologies I had been exposed to. He came away just as empty as I had.

Tommy's story recounted his rejection by the Methodist church and some years of leanness in his soul. Rejection is a powerful thing, he said, and to be rejected by one's peers and denominational leadership is very difficult to deal with. He spoke of his introduction to the healing movement. He talked about ministering with Agnes Sanford, Rufus Mosley, and E. Stanley Jones, who also influenced my life greatly. He spoke about Genevieve Parkhurst and many others of that movement, which later burst forth in the denominational churches as the charismatic renewal. It had been at that time, in 1949, through Oral Roberts, Billy Graham, Bill Bright and others, that a true renewal had broken forth. Although the denominational leaderships opposed it, as well as many seminaries, the people of God were being revitalized. By the time I came along, the breach between the people of God in the pews and the clergy had become a vast chasm.

Sociological Guinea Pigs

I recall having been told by the church members in Thomson that they were tired of being used as sociological guinea pigs for every new theology that came along. The fact is in my previous classes of theology and psychology, those who believed that God had absolutes concerning faith and practice were deemed unenlightened and to be pitied. Man had, in education, church, politics, family life, morality, and law, been re-enthroned as God. If you disagreed, you were to be avoided like the proverbial plague. Into such a theological world I had been born.

Tommy's story that morning rung deeply true for me and answered almost every question Barbara and I had asked the night before. We were impressed with the people we met at ORU and, by the end of the weekend, were looking for a way to continue my education there. Returning home and asking God to show us the way, both Barbara and I felt He was asking us to leave all that was familiar and, like Abram, "Go." He would show us the way. Within a few weeks we shared our hopes with the churches we were working with. They were extremely supportive about our going to Tulsa and to ORU. I informed my district superintendent, whose letter back to me was not at all encouraging. In fact, he warned me that Oral Roberts had money and, therefore, we should be suspicious of him. Along with this, our parents were mostly silent, but they did not try to dissuade us. A week or so later we had a garage sale and sold everything we could.

What little furniture remained was loaded into a small U-Haul trailer and, early in May, 1966, Barbara, Becky, Paul and I headed for Tulsa. I drove the U-Haul with Becky while Barbara drove our magnificent Studebaker with Paul. I remember Becky, who was then close to five years old, wanting to know how long it would take us to get there. Barb and I told her, "about fourteen Captain Kangaroos," and that seemed to satisfy her. We made it to Tulsa in about fourteen hours, arriving late in the afternoon, both scared and excited at the same time. We had a total of $189, no place to live, no job, and I had not been accepted in school. We prayed, asking God to help us, even if we had just done the dumbest thing in our lives, it being the only thing we had known to do to truly follow Him. As we drove by the beautiful, fledgling university campus, we noticed a sign about some apartments. After seeing the school, we drove to the apartments and found we could move right in. We did. We unloaded and, tired and hungry, got something to eat and fell into bed, exhausted and scared, happy and excited.

I awoke early the next morning and returned the U-Haul. About a half mile away was a Safeway grocery store where I stopped and applied for a job. They hired me on the spot, and I started as a sack boy the next morning. I also worked nights, stocking shelves. I remember, at the end of the first week, coming home feeling like Daniel Boone, with day-old milk, bologna and bread. Barbara was busy converting our little apartment into a home, something she has always done so beautifully. Soon, we were meeting other people in the complex. We heard that a Full Gospel Business Men's

Fellowship meeting was to take place in downtown Tulsa at the
Mayo Hotel. Anxious for all of God we could find, we decided
to go.

On our way to the meeting, we stopped at the bus station
for coffee. I noticed the sweetest looking man across from us.
He smiled so I asked him if he knew where the Mayo Hotel
was. He said he did, was going there himself, and would be
glad to show us the way. We arrived at the meeting and all
three of us sat together. As soon as the meeting started, one
of the men on the platform looked right at Barbara and me,
and I wondered what he could want. My question was soon
answered when he said, "Dr. Robert Frost is here. What a
privilege! Would you please come to the podium and give us
a word of greeting and pray for the meeting?" The man whom
we had met in the coffee shop rose to his feet, making his way
to the podium. There was much hugging and welcoming and it
was then I found out who he was. He was the new head of the
Department of Science at ORU and had just moved to Tulsa
himself.

We soon became aware that this was a fine man of God, and
a relationship developed that was to be a lifesaver for Barbara
and me. The meeting and the prayer ministry that Dr. Frost led
blessed us greatly. It was so gentle and yet powerful. After the
meeting he walked with us back to where our cars were parked;
and, before we parted, we stopped at his car and he gave us
a new book he had just finished writing, entitled *Aglow with
The Spirit.* That book proved to be filled with deep and helpful
insights concerning this new life we had just embarked on at
ORU. That night we returned, deeply encouraged and ready for
whatever God might have for us.

On my first day off I went to the school registrar and
registered for the fall semester. I was surprised to learn that
a friend from my days in Evanston, Floyd Kalber, had sent
a $1,000 gift for me. I met Floyd when, as a youth pastor in
Evanston, I heard that he spoke to youth groups about his life

and faith. Floyd was then high-profile in the TV business, being NBC's man in Chicago. He gave the nationwide news at 12:55 each day as well as national evening news. Floyd graciously came to our church and spoke to our young people. After this meeting he invited me to come down to the Merchandise Mart where the NBC studios were and have lunch with him. After that, I had many excellent conversations with him over lunch. Later, when I was appointed to the three churches on the Mississippi River, he graciously agreed to come speak on Layman Sunday in the Thomson Church. What a blessing he was and what a surprise to the congregation to hear such a fine man.

I was also able to qualify for a little money left on my G.I. bill. All in all, I was ready for school in the fall, having signed up for eighteen credit hours. I wasted no time in checking to see if there was any Methodist Church I could serve in Tulsa. I contacted the District Superintendent and scheduled a meeting with him. When I met him in his home, the first question he asked me was, "Are you one of those tonguers?"

By then I was learning how to respond to attacking questions about my experience. I said, "Sir, I am a Christian in the fullest meaning of that word; and, yes, I do speak in tongues!" He said how sorry he was, but there would not be any place for me in the Oklahoma Conference. I was saddened because I loved the life and ministry of John Wesley. I loved the hymns that he and his brother, Charles, had written. I had grown to love Methodism's roots and its expansion into America through Francis Asbury and Thomas Cokes, the first Methodist bishops in America. I read their diaries and all the history of that movement I could get my hands on. I even learned that an ancestor of mine, Peter Cartwright, had started and served the very circuit I served in Illinois. He also ran against Abraham Lincoln for state representative.

Suffice it to say, I loved the Methodist Church and her roots. I was deeply saddened the more I read of Methodism's history, feeling that the church had been high-jacked by cultural worshippers of education and "avant-guard" theologies that came and went like the seasons. No wonder the Methodist church was in such disarray among her members. The distance continued to grow between the denominational leaders and the pew sitters and financial resources. Many felt that their churches, schools, seminaries, hospitals, missions, and Sunday school curriculum, had been sold out to relativism and universalism. Retrospectively speaking, I am still aghast how little I heard about Jesus and the Christian life. Later in my Christian life I repented of my harsh judgment against the Methodist Church, having said in my testimony that I never heard the gospel there. Later, Paul Waters would sit me down in the sanctuary and play a great hymn, and then say, "Tom, we did hear the gospel in the hymns."

God's Mercy Never Fails, Even When Men Do

It was at this time we met another couple that I'll call John and Mary, who were attending ORU. Barbara and Mary became fast friends and I soon became friends with John. They were a Pentecostal couple who opened more doors for us into the world of Full Gospel Christianity. One day Barbara and Mary got the great idea of renting a house together. Barbara had gotten a job at a local credit union, allowing me to go to school full time. We were paying a nursery to watch Becky and Paul and we could save that money if Mary stayed home and watched our kids as well as her own. John was taking only six hours of classes and also working. Between his job and Barbara's, we could manage to rent a house.

After figuring out the financial savings, we rented a house together about three and a half miles from ORU. I signed the contract and we moved in, just after the start of the fall semester. The first several weeks went pretty well until my daughter Becky complained of some incidents concerning eating and John's discipline methods. It turned out there were some issues that needed to be resolved. When we couldn't come to agreement on them I proposed that one of the two families should move out. The next day they were gone. To this day, we have never seen them again.

During the interim between the couple leaving and our moving out of that house, I was contacted by a church in North Tulsa, asking if I might be interested in being an associate pastor in charge of the youth and evangelism. I met with the Pastoral Relations Committee and they approved but wanted to talk to the local District Superintendant as well as the one from Illinois. The Superintendant from Illinois told the church that I had had affairs, stolen money and was off in some kind of weird theology and couldn't be trusted. I was shattered. I could never recall being so openly lied about in my life, especially from a church leader. The Pastoral Relations Committee met again, now very concerned, and put off hiring me.

I had recently met a man at ORU who was to become a lifelong friend. Dr. Charles Farah was a seminary professor at ORU's seminary, whom I had met through Tommy Tyson. I called him and told him how hurt I was and how unjust the situation seemed. He hesitated on the phone and, after about thirty seconds or so, slowly replied, "Forgive them and ask God to make a way." I hung up, not feeling very comforted; but Barb and I did pray. The next day Charlie Groves, the pastor of Centenary United Methodist Church, called and said that the committee had unanimously decided to hire me anyway and asked when I would be available to move into a small house in north Tulsa and begin my work there. A parishioner owned a little house about a mile from the church and he rented it to us for $50 a month. We moved the next weekend and I began work in the church, which was a delight. I found out that Charlie Groves, a man in his early sixties was a "spirit-filled" Methodist minister and had faced some challenging denominational judgments himself.

We all loved the little house. Becky was enrolled at a school about two blocks away and we found Mrs. Pease, a wonderful woman of about seventy, to watch Paul during the day and to be there when Becky came home from school. I could return to school and Barbara continued her work at the credit union downtown. During this period we had several significant experiences.

I had started school carrying about seventeen hours in Psychology, Science, and English. Because of meeting Dr. Frost and going to that FGBMFI meeting, I was involved as a volunteer to help bring a similar seminar to Tulsa. Dr. John Tuel, head of the Psychology Department at ORU, called a meeting. We met at his home along with two other men. One of the men gathered there was Tink Wilkerson, a Tulsa car dealer, and a third man, Dr. Ray Long, head of the English Department at ORU. There I was with three professors and a car dealer. Over the weeks of planning we were invited to a prayer meeting at another ORU professor's home. I felt very privileged to be invited as Barbara and I had prayed for older brethren who could teach us.

Through these contacts I was asked if Barbara and I would like to attend a private, home meeting with a couple who were coming through town that week. We were thrilled to be asked and thought together, "Wow, someone who has been 'in the Spirit' for twenty-five years will be awesome to hear." We could hardly wait for the night to come. One of Dr. Frost's daughters babysat for us, and we arrived a little early with great expectations. I noticed that Ruth Frost, Dr. Frost's wife, was alone and that she stayed on the fringe of the fifty or so people gathered. After the owners of the home introduced the couple as having a proven ministry of long standing, the couple stood in front of the fireplace and began to tell us about their ministry. They called it The Ministry of Godly Rebuke. Barbara and I, being new in the spirit, could hardly wait for the meeting. Just before they began to give instructions and teaching about their ministry, I noticed Ruth Frost quietly leave. I didn't think much about it at the time, but would remember it later.

Their ministry began. Everybody had to be down on their knees with their eyes closed and the man would walk by each of us and pray in tongues over us. Behind him, his wife would come and give the interpretation of the tongues spoken over each. The interpretation would be "the Lord's rebuke" to our lives and would reveal how we could improve our walk and be more mature and spiritual. To refuse the rebuke was to risk offending God and be on the path to ruin. After you received your rebuke, they would then pray a prayer of confession and repentance over each of us for cleansing and renewal. When they prayed over me and I heard the interpretation, I was absolutely devastated. Many were crying out for prayer and deliverance from their black hearts and devious thoughts. I found myself walking to our car with hopelessness written all over my face. We went home, paid the babysitter, and silently went to bed. Barbara arose the next morning and, without a word concerning the night before, went off to work. I took Paul to Mrs. Pease' and saw Becky off to school.

As I drove from our house in North Tulsa slowly southward toward the campus, each mile seemed darker and gloomier. I arrived on campus and soon found myself at Dr. Frost's office. His office door was open and, seeing me, he graciously invited me in. As I walked in he said, "What in the world is the matter with you?" I told him how, at the meeting the night before, God had told me how horrible and black my heart was and that, if I didn't do what these people told me, I was headed for God's rejection and hell. He listened quietly for about fifteen seconds and suddenly came from around behind his desk and, taking my face in his hands, said, "Tom, during that ministry, did you feel love, joy, peace, acceptance and encouragement?" I said, "No! I felt rejected, unclean, immoral, dirty, and unworthy." He then said, "Does that sound like Jesus?" He continued by asking if I could recall Jesus ever treating anyone like that?" I replied, "No." Then Dr. Frost asked me if my spirit, down deep in my belly, agreed with what was being said and all that was going on? I said it had not, but I dismissed it because these people had a twenty-five year proven ministry. Who was I, so new to the Spirit, to question those older and wiser?

At this point, with great love and intensity, Dr. Frost looked me in the eye and said, "Tom, the Lord Jesus Christ has given you the Holy Spirit to dwell within you and to guide you into all truth. You will always know His presence by an inner witness. That is what He was telling you last night. The Holy Spirit does not scream and yell. His voice is tender and confident, peaceful, and always points to Jesus. The Holy Spirit does not threaten nor intimidate. If He has something to say, He will present it to you clearly and calmly. You then will be free to make your decision about it." He went on to say that it is the devil that comes to steal, kill, and destroy.

At that point, he calmly and firmly laid his hands on my head and prayed, "Father, I stand against the lies that the enemy of Tom's and Barbara's souls was trying to put upon them last night. Wash him, Holy Spirit, and free him from this condemnation that has no place in you." He went on, further, to declare, according to the scripture in John 3, that the Son of God didn't come to judge or condemn but to love and bless and that the previous night had been an attack against the freedom that Jesus had purchased for me and Barbara. "Now," he continued praying, "let it return and let them be free from this condemnation, in the name of Jesus, Amen!"

When he was finished praying my heart was singing and rejoicing. Dr Frost then told me that his wife had left the meeting as she discerned that this ministry was not of God. She also knew it was neither the time nor place for her to confront it, so she just left quietly. She told her husband she was particularly concerned about the impact it might have upon Barbara and me as well as others. She prayed all the way home, asking God to lead us and any others so that our walk with the Lord would not be hampered, but that God would turn it into a blessing. I had to agree that is just what He had done.

We talked for a few more minutes, and I left his office with joy, nearly sailing home after classes to tell Barbara about the condemnation that had come to us "in the name of the Lord."

I am very grateful for that experience as over the years I have been much more attuned to the inner voice. I have been saved countless times from following a pagan and siren call of the devil. Barbara and I have also been able to help scores of people learn that our Lord Jesus has given us a clean and good heart. Over the days, weeks, months, and years since then we have learned many lessons that have enabled us to smell when something is just not quite kosher. We have learned that believers of all ages should be very cautious of what kind of spiritual food they take in.

Good Morning, Brother Pilgrim

After about a semester at ORU, I was informed that they were looking for someone to work at the University's radio station, KORU, a 100,000-watt FM station. I was quite interested, tried out for, and got a job of announcing and doing some programming on the station. I fell in love with radio and realized I wouldn't mind doing this for a living. Little did I realize that within a year, through some unbelievable circumstances, I would become KORU's General Manager, announcer for Oral Roberts' radio program, and be on the air from 6 AM until Noon. I initiated a program called *Good Morning, Brother Pilgrim.* This program opened up a life and ministry I never dreamed of. The program aired five days a week from 6 to 6:30 a.m. I used Oral Robert's *Daily Blessing Devotional*, read other scriptures and prayed over the radio for requests that came in. It was through this program that eventually people started calling in to request I come and teach a Bible study in their home. This was the start of what was later to grow into Bread of Life Ministries.

Chapter 19

THE VOICE SPEAKS AT THE OSAGE
APARTMENTS 1966

W<small>HEN</small> I <small>WAS</small> serving at Centenary Methodist church in
North Tulsa with Charlie Groves, we introduced some
innovative new programs that got us in the newspapers. One of
my jobs was to call on the people in the church's neighborhood
and find ways to serve them. Charlie had been deeply touched
by the charismatic movement of the late 50s and early 60s so
we had similar hearts and experience.

'Community servants,' from left the Rev. Charles Groves, Elam Blank and Tom Mohn

The neighborhood
was "old" Tulsa
in that most of the
money in town had
moved south of
there. The result
was a lot of rundown
homes and lower
income families. Also
included in this area
was a housing project
called the Osage Apartments. This was government housing
with mostly blacks and a scattering of whites, Latinos, and
Indians living there. I went from apartment to apartment where
I found a real openness among the people. I asked several of
them if I could hold a religious meeting in their homes. I was
excited at the prospects. Sadly, after consulting with the church
board, it was decided that it would be much better if the people
would come to the church building instead. Charlie and I were
very disappointed and felt we had missed a great opportunity.

During that same time my parents vacationed in Tulsa and my dad, who had become a believer at the age of 67, went with me on my rounds. While calling on people in the Osage Apartments on a very cold day, we met a family from Arkansas who had moved to Tulsa in hope of finding work. They were very disappointed and couldn't pay the rent on their little house nor could they pay for food or electricity. They were cold, hungry and disappointed. The family consisted of a mother and father, two children, and grandparents. To say they looked pathetic and defeated when we met them is an understatement.

—World Staff Photo
Mohn, Gregory examine new 'Acts'

'The Church' Begins Again

"We're just going to call it 'The Church'," the Rev. Tom Mohn, community minister of Centenary Methodist Church, said enthusiastically of the most recent step taken by the congregation he serves.

Since Mohn, a ministerial student at Oral Roberts University, was employed at Centenary, he has devoted a part of every day to calling in the neighborhood to determine the needs of the people who live around, but have not attended, the church.

"I've found people who needed food or clothing and people who needed healing," Mohn explained, "but mostly I have found people who needed love and some ordinary common sense about how to order their lives."

Here is where the lay members of Centenary will come in. "We're inviting any member with any talent to come in Tuesday nights," said Mohn. "No pressure will be applied, but I've explained to the people that we can use every one of them.

"If a woman has no skill other than keeping house, caring for children or managing on a shoestring, I have found people who need that very kind of assistance."

Mohn believes it was this kind of simple help to one's fellow man that characterized the New Testament Church.

After hearing their story, Dad and I went back to the church and got several bags of groceries from the church along with a little money to pay for heat. We wished we had more but it was at least something. Upon receiving our gifts, the family expressed gratitude and we prepared to leave. The mother stopped us and asked if there was a doctor in our church who could look at their little girl. When we asked what was wrong, the mother called the little ten year old over to us and showed us her inflamed and infected dripping eye.

The little girl was pale, emaciated, and frightened. As I gathered her up in my arms, I heard the inner voice say, "Pray for her." I asked Dad to join me in prayer and laid my hand on her infected dripping eye. I said, "Jesus, you love this girl so much; heal her eye and let her know you will never leave her or her family."

Instantly the little girl squealed with delight and cried out, "I'm fine, I'm fine. I can see, and all the stuff is gone!" We all rejoiced and marveled at the miracle. Everyone looked at the little girl and her perfect eye. The whole family brightened up and the Dad said, "Let's go back to Arkansas. I just know everything is going to be alright."

We laughed and talked and prayed God's blessing on them and left. When I went back the following day they were gone. Dad, who had been skeptical about the charismatic renewal and had questioned our move to Tulsa to be part of it, never again had any doubts about what we'd done. He would later come to spend the final years of his life with us as a sweet and loving father, grandfather and father-in-law. Not only that, he would later teach in our school and bless many children with his godly patience and wisdom.

Chapter 20

DRIVING TO VIRGINIA

In the spring of 1968 Barbara and I were given the opportunity to become the chaplains in a girl's school in Virginia. This meant leaving ORU, and as we prayed we sensed that the Lord was leading us to accept the new challenge. So once again we sold most everything and headed out to Virginia in our now aging Studebaker. When we reached the first hills and then mountains of Tennessee and Eastern Kentucky we really prayed our little Studebaker would make it up the hills. As we drove into Kentucky a fog closed in on us and we feared driving further as trucks and cars were pulling over and waiting for a break in the weather.

Right then our whole family prayed, asking God to help us find a place to stay for the night that we could afford. As I had pulled off the road like many others, my daughter said, "Look Daddy your headlights are pushing away the fog." Sure enough I could clearly see the road ahead. I pulled the car back onto the highway and we proceeded on our trip. We noticed that all the other cars and truck were still on the sides of the road. Some looked at us as though we were crazy, yet I could see very clearly. Soon we came to a park sign and decided to go in and look for a lodge of some kind. As we drove in we were amazed at the beauty. We drove for about ten minutes and came to a lodge. There was one car there and very few lights on.

I parked the car and went into see if we could have a room. I was disappointed to find out that they weren't opening for several more days. It was a brand new lodge and the person I talked to could see my disappointment. I turned to walk out when he said, "Wait a minute, there's no one else here, go pick any room and stay the night".

I gladly accepted. We quickly unloaded and found a beautiful room overlooking a rolling vista. We settled in for the night with me hoping I had enough money to pay for the room in the morning. As the morning sun entered our room we all took baths, cleaned up and prepared for breakfast somewhere on the road. I went downstairs to pay the bill. When I asked the man what the cost was, he said "No charge, we aren't open for business so I can't charge you." He said he was glad to have had some company as he had been there all alone for several days. We said our many thanks and headed for Virginia, rested and grateful for what we felt was the care and mercy of God.

We had now definitely entered mountain country and I began to pray that our little car could make it up and down the dizzying road. I was really concerned as even in Tulsa I sometimes had to use the lowest gear to go up any hill. Becky our eldest was sitting in the front seat with Barbara and I when she said pointed to the temperature gauge and asked, "Daddy why is it way over on the H?"

I told her that meant the engine was overheating and we would have to wait until it cooled down to continue. Unfazed, she continued, "Daddy if Jesus can get us through the fog and get us a free place to stay, can't He cool the car down?"

Before I could answer, she and the family began to pray. Amazingly, we all watched the temperature gauge go down. Not only that, we also watched as I was able to go through the mountains in second and third gears. As soon as the car began to heat up again everyone would pray, rain would begin to fall and down the gauge would go. This happened all the way through the mountains until we finally arrived at our destination in Virginia. Another wondrous thing!

My two oldest children never forgot these experiences and still remind us of our miracle drive to Virginia. We were there for three months before receiving a call from Tommy Tyson asking us to return to Tulsa. The General Manager position at KORU had opened up and I was offered the job. So back we headed over hill and dale to the radio station at Oral Roberts University.

Chapter 21

DEALING WITH A SPIRIT OF PRIDE

AFTER WE RETURNED to Tulsa from Virginia, I became the general manager of KORU-FM radio station, working closely there with Oral Roberts, himself. I was able to renew some relationships that had started during the previous year. Dr. Tuel and Dr. Frost invited me to join them in a weekly prayer time they had with Dr. George Parkhurst, the attending psychiatrist at a local Psychiatric Foundation. His mother was Genevieve Parkhurst who was one of the pioneers in the healing ministry that expressed itself in the Camps Farthest Out Ministry. She was a prolific author, teacher, and conference speaker as well as having a powerful healing ministry. Dr Parkhurst was a member of First United Methodist Church.

Dr. Parkhurst and Dr. Tuel invited me to attend Monday afternoon prayer meetings and, again, I felt honored to be included and to learn from such truly godly men. After several months of attending each Monday at 5 p.m., I found myself about thirty minutes early one Monday. Dr Parkhurst had something he had to attend to and asked that I wait for him and the others in his office. He suggested, while waiting, I listen to a recording that had been made at a recent conference at a southern university. The recording was the story of a woman in Louisiana who had been in a catatonic state for several years. Her psychiatrist and others psychologists who had worked with her were presenting her case in this conference. They told of trying every kind of therapy, all to no avail. The husband of the woman asked if he could take his wife to a minister he had heard about to have him pray for her. The doctors agreed since they had exhausted everything they knew.

Her husband took her to a Baptist pastor who practiced deliverance ministry, i.e. casting out of demons. Over a period of time, he cast out seventeen demons from the woman. The woman was then presented to this conference at a southern university, sane and in her right mind. The doctors had no explanations or criticisms, just the woman's presence. The recording I was hearing was of one of the sessions that had been recorded by the Baptist pastor during one of his exorcism ministries. Dr Parkhurst thought I could learn something from this recording and he had it cued to a particular place that he wanted me to hear. In retrospect, he had discerned an issue in me that I was dealing with and wanted to speak into it. All this had the fingerprints of God on it.

The first thing I heard was the pastor talking to this woman and saying to her, "I am not addressing you. I am addressing the spirit. Spirit, I command you to come out." Out of this woman came a deep, male voice, saying he didn't have to because he had a legitimate right to be in her. The pastor said that he had no rights and must come out right then. The spirit replied, "Who are you to tell me to come out, and what authority do you think you have?" The pastor then said that ever since Jesus' death, burial, resurrection, ascension, and outpouring of the Holy Spirit, all true believers have His authority to cast out spirits. "So," he said, "you must come out by the authority of Jesus Christ."

At this point the spirit moaned and wailed and cried out, "Oh, ever since that time, we have been in trouble; our only protection has been ignorance and ridicule as to the truth of Him." The spirit then went on to say, "Why don't I come into you and I will make you the most sought-after spiritual leader in the entire South. People will come from all around to seek your wisdom and teaching. There will even be signs and wonders that you will do and many will marvel at the power. You will have a great ministry and will be very popular and wealthy."

Ignoring all that, the pastor told the spirit to leave and that he wanted nothing to do with his promises. With that, the spirit left and I could hear it screaming as it faded into the distance. At that point I stopped the recording. The whole portion had lasted only two or three minutes. I sat there a long time and pondered what I had just heard. As I did, I became very restless. I sensed anger rising in me, wondering why Dr. Parkhurst thought I ought to listen to this. After a few minutes, the others showed up and we had our prayer meeting. Neither Dr. Parkhurst nor I said anything about the recording.

As I drove home, I grew increasingly upset and angry, so much so that when I arrived home I wasn't fit company for anyone. The kids had already eaten dinner and were playing outside in the back yard. Barbara was ironing in the front room. She asked how the meeting had gone. Angrily, I told her about the recording and Dr. Parkhurst's comment that he thought I should hear this.

I was sitting on the couch right in front of the ironing board. When I finished my tirade, I folded my hands across my chest, expecting some understanding and compassion from Barbara. After a very long pause, she abruptly set the iron down and, looking me right in the eye, said, "You've heard that voice before haven't you? And not only that, you have been strongly tempted to heed it, haven't you?"

The fact is at this time God had opened up a teaching ministry for me called Bread of Life, and I was teaching several hundred people a week in small groups all over the city of Tulsa. I was also beginning to travel out of town and into other states for speaking engagements. There were some people who encouraged me to take my ministry nationwide. As a result, I had thought about promoting it with a singer, a platform man, and a road man to do the bookings. I looked at Barbara, shocked. She came around from behind the ironing board and, in the strongest voice I could recall her ever having used, said, "You foul spirit of false ministry, I command you to flee from Tom in the name of Jesus Christ. Neither he nor I want your ministry or your presence in our lives! Now GO!"

Instantly, my chest heaved and I felt a heavy, angry, burden leave and a lightness replace it. Within just a few moments I was once again at peace and rejoicing at the goodness of God.

Not long after this I was asked to leave a home in which I had held meetings for several months. This was the home of one of the people who had wanted to promote me nationally. Soon afterward this person, along with others, found someone else to promote. That ministry is now international. I only hope and pray that it isn't inspired from the wrong source as mine would have been. Once again, I thank God for the mentors He so lovingly gave us as we were growing in grace. As I remember these mentors, I am humbled by the fact that these relationships were gifts of God, none of them was pursued by me.

Other incidents that were significant took place after we had returned from Virginia in 1968. Barbara's father died at Christmas time and our son Tommy was born in April of 1969. A year and a half after that in 1970 we had a son Michael Christopher born prematurely and he died three days later. I tell that story in an upcoming chapter.

Chapter 22

WHEN "CONFESSION IS POSSESSION" FAILED

AT THIS TIME I was still working at KORU and also had begun teaching many groups throughout the city and elsewhere. It would be in March of 1971 that I would eventually leave ORU and go fulltime into the ministry we called Bread of Life.

In preparation for that, Barbara and I were being exposed to many new understandings of scripture and the Christian life. For instance we had witnessed personally many miracles of healing and deliverance so that we now knew through experience that Jesus truly is the same yesterday today and forever. He hadn't changed at all and could and would do everything that Scripture said he would. At this time the "confession is possession "movement was really going strong. Phrases like "The Bible says it, I believe it, I confess it, that settles it, and it will come to pass," became our mantras.

This teaching was very appealing to us. It allowed us to take our understanding of scripture and make it God's will. We decided therefore that it was always God's will to heal and if someone wasn't healed, it showed a lack of faith. We called that a negative confession. The other side of the theological road from the one we were on was called Cessationism. This said that God didn't do what he did in the book of Acts after the church was established. The miracles and gifts of the Holy Spirit ceased after the death of the last original apostle. The place I had come from theologically was that the miraculous gifts of the Spirit never really did take place. This position said that the Scripture was using hyperbole, or mythological language to describe events.

One who held this position could not trust the Bible in any kind of literal sense, and a person who did was suspect. At the same time the "God is Dead" theology was seriously studied as well as Situation Ethics which put forth that there are no moral absolutes. All truth is relative. There was also the revisionism of the writings of Dietrich Bonheoffer. He was reinterpreted to make it seem that when he spoke of religion-less Christianity he no longer placed credence in the Scripture or the born again experience. His strong evangelical faith was watered down to a social gospel devoid of the miraculous. His call to discipleship was so diluted that prayer, Scripture study, and fidelity to the Scripture was all but relegated to a less enlightened past age.

The positions of many who believed in a God who still acted in the human condition were considered simplistic at best and cultic at worst. I recall teachers in theology classes poking fun at students who had devotions, or memorized scripture, or who believed in miracles. I remember a Methodist minister walking down the center aisle of his church with the communion elements in a plastic bag and laughing that he had Jesus in a bag. On the other extreme I was also to meet believers and people of authority who worshipped the Bible in an equally unhealthy way and became Bibliolaters. All of these theologies were swirling around the church in the 1960's bringing confusion on every side.

At that time an event happened that showed us the shallowness of the way we were relating to the Lord and affected us forever. Barbara and I had been blessed with three children, a girl and two boys, when she became pregnant with our fourth child. In about her fourth month Barbara became concerned that something was different about this pregnancy. After seeing the doctor there seemed to be no concern although she sensed that something was not normal. This continued into the eighth month when her water broke and she went into labor early. The baby was born placenta previa and the doctor held out little hope for the baby boy to live. We named him Michael Christopher and early the next morning I baptized him.

As stated above, at this stage in our lives Barbara and I had been strongly drawn to the prevailing theology called "confession is possession." We believed that it was always God's will to heal as long as one persisted in one's confession and did not let in doubt or fear. As a result I only called people to pray for Michael's healing who had the same view and we all began to pray for healing.

The following morning Barbara called to tell me that Michael had died. I dressed quickly and very angrily drove to the hospital. During that approximately 15 minute drive I was overwhelmed with anger and confusion. We had only prayed with those of like mind that Michael would be healed. I am embarrassed as I remember the foul words I hurled at God for letting us down. Hadn't we prayed positively and faithfully? Hadn't we been faithful? Much more poured out of my mouth as I cursed God for having been unfaithful to us. In essence I believed that He owed us as we had been faithful in our confession.

I arrived at the hospital parking lot and sat in my car for a few minutes   As I sat there remembering all I had said in anger and sadness concerning the death of our son, I began to tremble with fear. After all I had said, surely God was now going to kill me. I literally sat there waiting to die. Time seemed to stop as I shook and waited. Several minutes passed and slowly I began to wonder why nothing seemed to be happening when out of my belly came these words, "Though He slay me yet will I trust Him." As these words rose to my mouth and consciousness, I began to sense a deep peace. I slowly began to recall the "voice in the belly" that God had led us by for several years. As I did, I gained my composure and went up to see Barbara with an unexpected joy to tell her what the Lord had shown me. When I arrived in her room some of the other women were nursing their newborns and I could sense Barb's disappointment. I bent over and embraced her and we cried together. For a few moments nothing was said; we just held each other and each of us prayed silently.

After a while I told her I had something to share that happened on my way to the hospital. She also had something to share with me that had happened after she had called me. She began by saying she had been bitterly sad and disappointed along with feeling anger toward God. As she shared these feelings with me I began to sense a presence. Barb went on to say that after she cried and expressed her concerns silently to God, she heard a voice from within saying, "Though He slay me, yet I will love Him." When she spoke I began to grin from ear to ear. When she looked at me in surprise, I responded by saying, "Sweetheart, I had the very same experience in the parking lot just minutes ago." We both began to feel our heaviness, confusion and anger lift. We embraced each other and began to thank God. We talked for a few more minutes and I left to go home with our other children.

When I arrived home a dear sister named Katharine who was watching our children sat with me as I told the kids about Michael's death and God's subsequent comfort. When the sister left she said she could return in the morning so I could go and pick up Barbara.

The next day arrived and Katherine came to watch the children. I went in to shower and prepare to go to the hospital. While I was in the shower I heard a loud voice singing, "There's a sweet, sweet Spirit in this place and I know it's the Spirit of the Lord." I turned the shower off and yelled at Katherine asking who it was that was singing. She yelled back, "Why Tom, it's you." I said I was not singing but she yelled

back that I was. I told her I was not and resumed my shower.
When I heard the same singing again, I shut off the shower
and again called out to Katherine. Her reply was the same. I
laughed and said, "Give me a break." I began the shower again
and heard the same song again. This time I realized it was, in
fact, coming from deep within me. I was the one singing and in
my wonder I sensed the deep presence of the Lord.

Just before I left for the hospital Katherine said she and
her husband Jim had been praying for us. The Lord brought to
their attention the time when David and Bathsheba had a child
who was ill and they fasted and prayed for him. Still, the child
died. David's response was to say, "But now he has died why
should I fast? Can I bring him back again? I shall go to him
but he shall not return to me." As I listened to Katherine I
realized again the faithfulness and love of God even when the
unexpected or sad events of life happen. I thanked her and left
for the hospital.

On the way I was excited about sharing Katherine's words
with Barb. But when I arrived she immediately sat up in bed
and started talking. She said she had been awakened early
in the morning and was drawn to the story of David and
Bathsheba when they lost their child even after praying and
fasting. I burst into thankfulness as she talked and quickly told
her of Katherine's words. Despite our deep sorrow, we were
both overwhelmed with a sense of the Lord's presence and
spent memorable moments in prayer together.

As we got ready to leave, the chaplain came into the room.
He was a compassionate young man and wished to console us
concerning our loss. As he spoke with great earnestness and
human concern both Barbara and I felt his desire to comfort
us. The truth was, he really didn't know how to comfort us.
We listened to him and as he concluded we expressed our
appreciation for his coming and his words and time. He seemed
to hesitate for a few moments and then noticed I was a pastor.
I sensed he was waiting for something else from us. I paused a

moment quietly asking the Lord what we might say. I told him that Jesus by His Spirit had comforted us in a most marvelous way. Then I shared with the chaplain the God experiences we had had over the past two days.

When I finished he looked at us and began to cry. When he regained control he asked us to pray for him. As we prayed, the young man melted before the Lord. When we finished he thanked us profusely saying he had never experienced the Lord's presence so powerfully. We assured him that this Lord was powerful, intimate and always present. The chaplain said thank you and remained in a prayerful state as we left.

On the way home we desired to share all that had happened with our children. We arrived home and thanked Katherine for her and Jim's revelation. We shared our experience with them and again the Lord overshadowed the time. About a year later Barbara would have an intense dream in which any lingering questions and confusion about the whole pregnancy and death would be washed away by the Lord's presence.

During the next few weeks as we further processed the events and insights God had given us, we re-evaluated our theology concerning not only healing but the teaching that what believers should always do was to find a scripture that would speak to any given situation and confess it. We felt a great deal of shame and anger at what had been taught to us about using God and the Bible in this way and that we had been so gullible in readily accepting that theology. Through that experience and subsequent years, our theology has been revamped again and again as we grew in our relationship with Jesus and His ever present Spirit.

As Barbara and I verbally and prayerfully brought our questions and confused theology before God, the Lord reminded us of many things He had so faithfully allowed us to read, hear and experience. We remembered E. Stanley Jones who had written many decades before about such things. In the one case he revered the Scriptures in a way that drove liberals crazy and in the other he refused to worship the Scriptures the way many evangelicals did. His position arose from his understanding that Jesus was the Word of God and that the scripture had to yield to His person, not the other way around. The written word would always be subservient to the Person of Jesus as The Word Incarnate and must bow before Him.

Jones' insight into John 5: 39-40, was particularly revealing. *"You search the scriptures, because you think that in them you have eternal life: and it is these that bear witness to me: and you are unwilling to come to me, that you may have life."* The Scriptures don't give life, Jesus gives life to them. This scripture and many others gave loving insight to the Person of Jesus as the Word and the place of the scriptures in relationship to him.

We were to see and lament many times over, the bad theology of "confession is possession," and the harm it would cause in the Body of Christ. We saw many people deeply wounded and discouraged, some who even ended up seeking reality in a variety of "isms" and outright demonic alternatives that the enemy uses to seduce wounded people. Through this experience and many others we were drawn directly back to Jesus as the source of our theology and life. He stands above all else and is able to carry us through all of life's experiences.

Chapter 23

A MIRACLE AND A REBUKE

TWO OTHER INSTANCES of God's speaking to me through the inner voice stand out from my time at KORU. You can imagine how important a broadcaster's voice is in broadcasting. I woke up early one morning with a bad case of laryngitis. I couldn't even squeak one word. I hurried to the university and went into the dorm to get some help from my student broadcasters only to find out that they were gone on a school holiday.

My thought was to go on the air and try to find an old tape or old *Good Morning Brother Pilgrim* devotional and hope I could get by with it. I turned on the station's power and prepared to sign on and begin the first program. As I looked for an old program, the voice deep in my belly said, "Trust Me, it will be alright." I thought this must either be the enemy desiring to make a fool out of me or it was the Lord asking me to trust Him. Thankfully, I chose the latter.

I watched the second hands on the studio clock click toward airtime. I put on the tape for the daily station opening and prepared for the devotional. When the on air tape finished I pressed on the microphone switch and said loudly and clearly, " Good Morning Brother Pilgrim." From then on throughout the 30 minute program my voice held strong and true. I finished with live prayer and then segued into the other morning programming. When I shut the microphone off and started to speak, I could hardly make a sound. This happened throughout the rest of the morning. Every time I needed to do a headlines newsbreak or station ID, I could speak just fine, but as soon as I was done, my voice was gone. I went off the air at noon and went home still very hoarse, amazed at how the morning had gone. This was another in the long list of wondrous things the Lord used to show me his goodness and power.

Perhaps a week or so later, as I went off the air to other programming I began to think about some decisions and practices that were going on at the University. I became incensed and very critical of President Roberts, the Deans, and other board members of ORU. I spouted off to God about how I felt and that He should deal with them. Instantly I sensed this clear and lovingly patient response, "When you have been as faithful to your call as Oral and the others have been to theirs we'll talk" That was over 40 years ago and the Lord and I have not broached the subject again. At this point in my life I see the folly of feeling it necessary to make judgments about which I know little or nothing.

Chapter 24

HOME MEETINGS SPRING UP

As a result of my radio program, people would invite me to come lead Bible Studies in their homes. The first Bible Study met in late November, 1968. Within a year the meetings had expanded to several each week.

The day came when I told my boss at KORU, Ron Smith, about my desire to go into a ministry of teaching. I quickly received a call from President Roberts asking if I would have breakfast with him and his wife Evelyn at their home. I gladly agreed and came the following Sunday morning. We enjoyed a wonderful breakfast, prepared by Evelyn, after which President Roberts asked about my thoughts about leaving KORU and starting a teaching ministry.

I told him how the decision had come about and that we felt this was how the Lord was leading us. His and Evelyn's response were incredibly tender. He said in no way did he want to have any part in me missing God's call for our lives. Nonetheless, he said that he had a job offer he wanted to present me with. The offer was absolutely marvelous. I must admit that the idea of staying on there at ORU and working with Oral Roberts was tempting, indeed.

Barb and I had prayed long and hard concerning our decision. Our conclusion was that we were as certain as we could be that the ministry of teaching was the call of God for our lives. I hesitatingly told President and Mrs. Roberts of our decision. I will never forget the tenderness and sweetness with which they responded. They said they completely understood our decision and fully supported us, having been in the same position themselves years before. They laid hands on me and prayed some of the most supportive and moving prayers I can ever recall. They blessed our path and calling, and affirmed us with tender prayer. We talked a few more minutes and then they gave me warm hugs and assured me the door would always be open if I wanted to return to ORU. I can say with conviction that their prayers for us are still being answered these many years later.

So it was that in March of 1971, I left ORU and KORU FM to go into full-time ministry. That ministry, called Bread of Life, was incorporated in 1970. By that time I held ten to fifteen meetings a week in the Tulsa area, teaching and speaking to more than a thousand people a week in small groups in homes all over the city and the surrounding area.

I had early morning meetings, afternoon meetings, and evening meetings. Many times I stayed late into the night, praying for, counseling, and ministering to people. Some of these evening home meetings would have one hundred or more people stuffed into one house. I recall one meeting that always had people sitting up the stairs, in the halls, and even in the bathroom.

Shortly thereafter, I started receiving invitations to speak and teach all over the Southwest. For several years I traveled to Little Rock every other weekend and had great meetings there as well as many other places in Arkansas, Texas, Louisiana, Kansas and Missouri. I also traveled every other weekend to McAlester and two smaller Oklahoma towns, Coalgate and Ada.

Ada was especially wonderful as we met in a Catholic home. The nuns from the Catholic school would come, and they were a delight. I even taught in their school in Ada on several occasions. There were five sisters who touched my life deeply with their passion for Jesus and the scripture as well as their tender loving care for children. I wished I had had such teachers growing up. The owners of that particular home in which we met owned a liquor store in Ada and were two of the most hospitable and gracious people I have ever known. The lady of the house always insisted that I come early so she could put on her best steak, potato, and salad for me. About twenty-five people would come from all denominations. The singing and fellowship was rich and deep.

The Coalgate meeting met in the home of the local school administrator. That meeting was characterized by many amazing miracles. A badly deformed arthritic knee was instantly healed. In one case a lowered shoulder, the result of a birth defect, was preventing a young man from entering the Air Force Academy. As we prayed for his shoulder, he was instantly healed, his shoulder literally thrusting my hand into the air as I prayed. A young woman of our acquaintance would often accompany Barbara and me as we drove to these meetings from Tulsa. She had been raised in California in a Pentecostal family, and she remarked after seeing one of these miracles that all her life things such as that only happened before or after she was there; now she had seen it first hand.

Such was the power of God in our midst.

Chapter 25

UNIVERSITY PROFESSORS FIND TRUE HEALING

I HAVE WRITTEN much about the voice of our Lord as the great Shepherd of the sheep. I learned to hear His voice in different and difficult situations.

During the Bread of Life years I went to Little Rock, Arkansas, every other week alternating with two other brothers from Tulsa. They were both charismatic but had a somewhat different theology than I did on listening for the Lord's voice. As we ministered to many of the same people some confusion was bound to arise. Such was the case in early 1973.

On one such trip I arrived and was greeted at the airport by two women. They asked if I had the time to visit a couple they had been witnessing to concerning healing. I said yes and we proceeded to the couple's home. On the way the women filled me in a little about the couple. They were both professors at the University of Arkansas and had both taught there for more than 20 years. These women had heard of the wife's long suffering with cancer. She had been fighting it for almost a year when these women talked to them about the desire of Jesus to heal her.

As we drove toward the home, my two fellow passengers lamented that the woman wasn't being healed because she was refusing to claim by faith her healing. As I listened I became uneasy and said nothing. I began to ask the Lord i.e. the Voice within me, what might be going on. We arrived at their home where I was introduced as a man of God who prayed for the sick. The couple warmly welcomed me. I quickly sensed that

I needed some time alone with the couple. I suggested that the women who had brought me return in a hour or so and pick me up. They had other errands to run so agreed and went on their way.

As soon as they were gone I asked the couple to tell me about their teaching experiences. They both excitedly told me of their mutual love of learning and teaching. They said that the students meant so much to them as they were unable to have children and the students more than filled that emptiness. For many minutes they regaled me with stories of interaction with students and the joy this brought to them. They felt their lives were full and meaningful. As they talked I became more aware of the effects of the cancer on her and of the husband's great concern and love for his wife. She was grey and weak and in a housecoat.

Although she came alive talking about their lives as professors, she soon displayed grave weakness. He moved close to her and embraced her tenderly. He mentioned that the cancer was getting worse and that they would sure love a miracle. As I spoke with them they never mentioned any religious experience or church relationship. I opened the subject by asking if or where they fellowshipped. Their answer was they had been married in church years ago but had never attended one after their wedding.

The women who brought me had heard about the professor through a student and had spoken to him about the Lord and healing. The professors didn't know much at all about the women except that the ladies seemed concerned about her health. The result was that the women had prayed for her and had frequently encouraged her to claim her healing. This was confusing to both of them. I listened to their appreciation for the women's concern and also their quandary about what it meant to claim healing.

At the same time I was inviting the voice within to speak

to me. I was at a loss not knowing how or even if I should pray for her. The Lord began to lead me to ask some basic questions. I asked if they had ever had a relationship with Jesus. They said no and weren't sure what that meant. I explained a little of my own testimony of growing up in the Methodist church and serving as a pastor for four years before I even knew one could know Jesus personally with profound and deep assurance. They were surprised and interested and began asking questions about God, faith, Jesus and church.

As best I could I answered each question simply and briefly. After about 20 minutes they both eagerly asked if they could enter into a relationship with God right then! I said, "Sure."

I very simply prayed with them giving them opportunity to make their own confessions and acceptance of Jesus. No sooner had we prayed when a tangible peace filled them and the house. They smiled big smiles and began to cry with joy and thanksgiving. The whole experience had been so simple and real. I shared with them that Jesus was the same yesterday today and forever; that they could talk to Him at anytime. I spent a few minutes going over John 10 with them, explaining that His sheep hear His voice and they were now His sheep. He also could and would hear them. Excitedly we prayed, first thanking the Lord for His obvious presence and then for her healing.

No sooner had we finished praying when the two women arrived back to take me to my meeting. The two professors joyfully shared what had happened. They profusely thanked me and soon we were on our way.

I finished the weekend of meetings and returned to Tulsa. The following Monday I was beginning one of the weekly home meetings we had there when the phone rang. It was the professor from Arkansas wanting to speak with me. He first thanked me for meeting with him and his wife. He then quickly and somewhat shockingly told me she had died that morning.

I immediately expressed my sympathy and told him we would pray for the Lord to be with him through his loss.

Again he thanked me but then quickly said, "Perhaps you don't understand. I am grieving the death of the love of my life but it's O.K! Jesus has been with me and my wife through the whole time. I know we will one day be together again. You, Tom, may never know how much your visit meant to us. We could never have made it through her last 24 hours without Jesus. He has been and, I know, will continue to be with me as I grieve and await our reunion." A few more words were said. As I placed the receiver back on its cradle I heard the voice say, "Rejoice, I have healed them both."

I have never forgotten this incident and I am continually reminded that truly *"Our God causes all things to work together for good,"* Romans 8:28.

Chapter 26

THE VOICE GUIDES IN LITTLE ROCK

DURING THE EARLY years of the Bread of Life ministry
I spent a lot of time on the road speaking at weekend
conferences. A friend in Little Rock, Arkansas, had organized
a meeting there for me. He rented a meeting room in the
Lincoln Hotel. He forewarned me that many of the people who
were coming desired to hear new teaching on the Pentecostal
experience of the Baptism of the Holy Spirit. My friend, being
a Baptist, said that many of the attendees were from Baptist
churches and were skeptical of the Holy Spirit experience.
Some churches had even sent deacons to listen and question
me. Some had agreed to come having heard I had been a
Methodist minister. Given the difficulties I had experienced
with such people before, I was filled with apprehension.
Nonetheless, the Lord had opened a door there and I believed I
should walk through it.

There were about 150 people present as we began the
meeting with some good Baptist hymns. The room was set up
so that there was a wide center aisle. I had prayed and written
some notes about what I thought I might say. As I stood up
to speak, I looked at the notes. In that moment, they seemed
meaningless. I began to panic and inwardly cried out to the
Lord, "What shall I do, I have nothing to say and these notes
make no sense whatsoever."

All of a sudden, I heard laughter. At first I thought it was
coming from the audience. I looked around but could see that
no one out there was laughing. I quickly realized the laughter
was coming from the voice within me! As I listened to the
laughter a plan formed in my heart. I chuckled as I thought

about it. The plan simply was "Get down on your knees in the middle aisle and tell them you are going to show them how to roll on the floor in the Spirit."

I hesitated but realized I really had no other plan. Very slowly I walked from the podium to the front of the middle aisle. Looking the group over from right to left I said, "Let me show you how to roll on the floor in the Spirit." I then bent over and was almost on the carpet when I quickly got up and said "Gotcha."

The room erupted in laughter. It took a few minutes to regain everyone's attention but soon a gentle, peaceful, open attitude invaded the room. I then began by talking about the "promise of the Father" that Jesus spoke about in Luke 24 that the disciples were to wait for. I also talked about the ministry of the Holy Spirit in John 14-16. The audience opened up like teachable children and the morning, afternoon and evening meetings were full of joy. Question after question came from those present. Though I certainly could not answer them all, the dialogue was healthy and productive. Many said it had been one of the most helpful times they had ever had concerning the subject of the ministry of the Holy Spirit. As a result, most of them no longer considered Pentecostals and Charismatics as emotional fools, unwilling to truly study the scripture.

I was to have many more wonderful meetings with this group of people. God, by His Spirit, does do wondrous things and He has a marvelous sense of humor!

Chapter 27

THE LORD LENGTHENS A LEG

DURING THE CHARISMATIC renewal all sorts of strange things happened. They seemed to have no meaning other than God showing that He does whatever he pleases. Period! One such thing happened in a meeting when I was asked to pray for a man named Dick. His left leg was 2 1/2 inches shorter than his right. He showed us how he had to have his left shoe built up and talked about how expensive that was every time he bought new shoes.

I had heard of praying for leg lengthening and, honestly, was quite skeptical. It sounded to me like some sort of psychic manipulation, or chicanery. After we all looked at his built up shoe, I asked him to sit down in a straight back chair and extend his legs. I asked everyone there to look very closely as I held his heels open-handed in my hands. I wanted to make certain all could see I wasn't pushing or pulling, that I had no grip whatsoever.

We all began to pray. Immediately his left leg jumped out. Dick cried out, "Oh, my God, let me see if I can walk correctly." He got up and walked around the room. Pretty soon he was smiling and jumping. He then put on his old built up shoe and found he was tilting to the right. He began to laugh saying, "I can hardly wait to get a new pair of shoes." I have continued to know this man for over 30 years and he has never had to buy built up shoes again.

This ability to pray for legs to be lengthened went on for close to a year in my life. I experienced it several times, and then it just went away. I have asked God why that is, with no answer other than the one I began this story with. God does what He wants to do. Period! Oh, my magnificent, mysterious God!

Chapter 28

FAMILY BLESSINGS

THE LORD HAS shown his ever present love and care for our family throughout our entire life times. In the midst of all those years certain instances occurred that showed us in special ways the Lord's activity in our family. Here are some of those instances.

The Healing of an Eardrum

One day while I was working at KORU, an emergency call from Barbara forced me to hurry home from the station. Our daughter, Becky, had fallen off her bicycle and was bleeding from her ear. Barbara had gotten the call from a woman about a mile from our home and had no quick way to get to Becky since I had the car. I quickly raced home to find Barbara waiting in the driveway. With the address in hand we rushed to the home.

When we arrived the woman who had called us was cradling Becky in her arms. She quickly told us that Becky had been going very fast down a hill. She lost control of the bike and had tumbled over the bars, hitting her head as she fell. We picked her up and rushed her to the hospital.

Immediately the doctor took an X-ray while we waited for the diagnosis. During this time we were in the emergency room with Becky. As we waited Barbara and I laid hands on Becky's ear and prayed. We asked God to bless her and prevent any kind of hearing problem. The x-ray came back and showed a basal skull fracture. We had noticed that after we prayed the bleeding had stopped. We told the doctor about that and asked him to take another x-ray. Very hesitatingly he agreed, saying that it was unnecessary. He knew what the x-rays showed.

Amazingly enough, the second x-ray showed no damage at all. The thought then was that perhaps just a tiny blood vessel had ruptured which now was healed. The doctor, Barbara and I stared at one another. The doctor broke the silence with, "She looks fine to me; no treatment needed, let me know if there are any problems."

There never were. Thank you, Doctor and Jesus.

Tommy and the 220

In the midst of the ministry pressures we were experiencing, we also had some scary and amusing family experiences that showed us the grace of the Lord.

When our son Tommy was about 8 years old he was very curious. It was one of those very hot spells in Tulsa when the temperature had soared over 100 for several days in a row. At the end of one of those hot days, Barbara and I were hoping that the evening would bring some cooler temperatures and perhaps even a breeze. As the sun was setting; we noticed our air conditioner was running all the time. The older kids were getting ready for bed when we noticed the lights dimming off and on.

Barb and I thought we were going to lose power and would have to spend the night waiting for the local electricity company to repair our outage. As we bathed and prepared the older kids for bed, we noticed that Tommy wasn't in the house. I went looking for him. He wasn't in the front or back yard, so as a last resort I went into the garage.

To my surprise, there he was standing in a puddle of water playing with the fuses and the 220 volt receptacle for the washer and dryer. He was gleefully turning the fuses on and off and giggling at the light and dark that he was controlling. Much to his surprise, I leapt for him and grabbed him out of the water. He had no idea of the danger he had been standing in the midst of, or the great danger he faced of literally being fried. I held him so close I no doubt squeezed the breath out of him. I kissed him, and held him tighter and tighter. I realized he had no idea of how close he had come to death.

I rushed us both back into the house loudly thanking God and yelling to the rest of the family what had just happened. The older kids as well as Barbara joined me in gasps of thanksgiving. Meanwhile, Tommy was simply surprised by all the love and hugs he was getting. One again a miracle had taken place. "A wondrous thing" had happened that we will never forget.

Matt and Six Year Old Wisdom

This family story is not a miracle in itself but it did teach me a life lesson about how sometimes we put the cart before the horse in our thinking about how God works. Our youngest son Matthew was a lover of hard boiled eggs. As a result Barb would hard boil a number of eggs for him, write an H on them and place them in the refrigerator at a level that Matt could reach. Quite often Matt would go to the refrigerator looking for eggs with his mother's "H" marked on them. He would confidently take one with an H on it out, crack it, and enjoy it thoroughly.

One morning he looked in the frig and found no eggs with an H on them. No problem. He simply pulled out a fresh egg, got himself a marker and wrote an H on the egg as he had seen his Mommy do many times. He then went to the sink, and proceeded to crack and peel the egg. He was absolutely shocked to watch the raw egg break apart and fall through his fingers into the sink. His response was classic; he called for his mother to come and fix the marker so he could get a hard-boiled egg.

Sounds a bit like some wrong headed Christian thinking, doesn't it! We think we can change the inside by just putting the right kind of mark or label on the outside. But it doesn't work. Real change has to come from the inside out, from where Jesus lives, not the other way around.

Barbara and the Seizures

Barbara and I took a trip to our hometown of Rockford, Illinois in the Spring of 1977. During that time we stayed at my folk's home. We slept in a bed which was smaller than the king sized one we had at home in Tulsa. During the night Barbara turned over and slipped off the side of the bed, hitting her head on the corner of a table. I awoke to her cry and saw to my shock that she was convulsing.

I immediately called out for my Dad and Mom to come and help us. When Barb stopped the serious shaking, we picked her up and took her to the hospital. She was unconscious and remained that way for about four hours. When we could finally talk with the doctors, their diagnosis was that the fall had caused her to have the seizures. Their opinion was that she would probably need epileptic type drugs for the rest of her life. Naturally that was very depressing news.

Barbara had another seizure before we left Rockford and headed home to Tulsa. We laid her in our VW van as she still had migraine-like headaches. I got her home where we had a local neurologist look at her. That doctor continued to prescribe strong anti-convulsive drugs. During the following months, Barbara, who was pregnant for much of that time, had several grand mal seizures. Needless to say, the seizures really scared me. The neurologist said that we may have to increase her drugs.

During the next few months I had difficulty sleeping. In fact, I found myself afraid to sleep. The thoughts that crowded in on me at night were sullen and depressing. Our concerns for the unborn baby continued to grow. It was in Barbara's 7th month of pregnancy that we felt drawn to attend a meeting in Oklahoma City. There were altogether about 15 people there. During the meeting we were standing in a circle and worshipping. Our hands were in the air as we sang, prayed, and praised the Lord.

All of a sudden Barbara turned to me and said, "I'm healed."

A big smile broke out on her face but she didn't say anything to anyone else. We decided to see the neurologist as soon as we could. Upon arriving home and making an appointment, the doctor gave her an EEG. He said that there had been a change in her results. He said that he would slowly reduce the meds to see if she truly was seizure free. Over the next three months he reduced the meds, and, the reality was, Barbara was drug free. She has never had a seizure since then, now over 35 years ago. Our daughter Sarah, who was born beautiful, strong, and healthy in June of 1977, is a living reminder to us every year of the wondrous thing the Lord did for us that summer.

What an amazing God He is!

Early Interventions and Reassurances

Here is an experience Barbara had that revealed God's deep love for our family to her.

"From the time of my second birth till now, I've never been alone. Jesus is with me as an unobtrusive friend. I am never lonely, and rarely afraid. My temptation to be anxious arises when those I love make decisions whose consequence will likely be harmful. Then I remember how God has used my impulsive willfulness to work out His perfect plan for my life, and my fears dissipate. This assurance of His constant presence came in the months following my conversion.

During the birth of our second child, in the final stages of delivery, I cried out to my new friend and He became a spiritual anesthetic covering me like a warm blanket. I had a pain-free natural birth. Our son, Paul, was the first-born in our land of promises fulfilled. I, along with his dad and big sister, welcomed him with joy.

In Thomson, our home was located on the main highway

through the tiny town of less than 500. Becky loved to ride her rusty little tricycle out on the front sidewalk as the cars sped by. Across the highway a gentle, white mare would feed in a fenced pasture. Becky loved that horse. I was terrified she would forget our admonitions and venture across the highway. I prayed and pleaded for the Lord to protect her, but I could not come to a place of peace. I had faith that He was with me, but I didn't believe He was with her. My fear was evidence of that. I knew intuitively that this fear was not from Him so I prayed, "Lord, I'm afraid for my kids. I'm terrified I won't be able to protect them. Help me!"

A few nights later, exhausted by the stress of trying not to worry, I fell into a sound sleep. The Lord gave me a beautiful dream: We were walking together--- Becky's hand in mine and three-month old Paul securely perched on my hip. It was a glorious, spring day, and we were enjoying a stroll through a field abounding with flamboyant wild flowers. In the distance I saw a man sitting on an outcropping of rock. As we came closer, he turned and gazed at me. Liquid love poured from His eyes into my spirit. It was the Lord Jesus. Paul leaned toward Him and Becky ran to Him. He scooped them both into His arms with such joyful acceptance that I was almost envious. Then He looked at me again, and, without words, He communicated in living words to my heart. "I love them more than you know. They are safe with me. Be at peace."

I slept peacefully that night and every night following. This encounter enabled me to entrust my children to God's care, no matter their age or location. Looking back, I can see His unending faithfulness to be with them, comfort them, discipline them, and protect them without my intervention.

Chapter 29

THE SHEPHERDING MOVEMENT

WE BECAME INVOLVED in the Shepherding movement that was popular in the US in the 1970's mainly because of Bob Mumford whom we had met in 1968. Bob filled a great need in our lives as a role model and spiritual mentor. Much could be said about the Shepherding/Discipleship movement and its demise. I wish however to only speak of my own failures during this time. Those who began the movement were men of God. My roots with many of those men went back to the mid-1960's when we were just starting out in our experience of the Charismatic movement.

I first heard Derek Prince in Chicago at a six hour deliverance service in a Pentecostal church, right after we were saved in 1965. I saw things I had only read about in Scripture. Barbara prayed in the Spirit the whole time while I went up front and watched as demonic manifestations occurred. These included Satanic voices, convulsions, and the sound of spirits leaving people and wailing as they departed. It was an unnerving but a powerful experience. Derek's first wife ministered with him in Dutch with great insight and power. They never raised their voices but spoke with great authority.

I met Charles Simpson at a meeting I attended at a Full Gospel convention in 1965. At that time he was a young pastor of a Baptist church in Pascagoula, Alabama. Charles was a delightful man whom I got to know rather well even before the movement started. Before and after the movement began he along with Derek and Bob Mumford came to Tulsa many times.

I met Bob Mumford in 1968 while serving as chaplain in a girl's school in Virginia. He was a pastor at a little Pentecostal church in Wilmington, Delaware. Before and after the shepherding time we became good friends. Although I've not seen him in many years I still count him as a friend and a fine man of God. To this day I still hold in high regard these brothers who tried honestly and desperately to bless the body of Christ. Most of the abuse of authority did not come from them but from those with delegated authority who were over lower level people like me. I was given wrong-headed leadership by those directly above me and so were many others. Sadly I passed on what was modeled to me. Eventually Bob repented, as did Derek, to those they had been overseeing.

Why did the Shepherding Movement get started? These men had seen many previous renewals come and go with little if any lasting effect. Their intention was to provide more structure to those in their care with the hope that this would lead to more lasting transformation. Sadly, in the long run, it did not turn out that way.

The authority structure that was created around me and people like me was not healthy due to our own innate, sinful, desire to exercise control over other people's lives. The way the structure was set up, the local shepherd had authority over the local flock in all things. As one of those local shepherds, I also appointed leaders under me who, like me, had little or no true understanding of authority. We, in essence, became little popes over those in our authority structure, dictating how they should live their lives in our attempt to correctly guide them.

My leaders and I governed the lives of the flock in every area: their marriages, child rearing, finances, relationships, jobs, and so on. We forgot that that the Scriptures said in Isaiah, "The government shall be on HIS shoulders," speaking prophetically of the Lord Jesus alone. As I look back, I can see that we were truly meddling in people's lives. We thought, of course, we were doing it for their own good and growth. I tremble as I remember the lives that were damaged. When I left the movement I spent at least two years going to people and repenting. Some forgave me, others did not. Some forgave me years later. Many who were wounded were not directly wounded by me but by the ones I had put over them. I learned that as the captain of the ship, I still was responsible for the mistreatment some of them received. To this day, as I remember the hurt and pain I directly allowed, I am grateful for the Lord's forgiveness. Through his grace, I no longer live with regret.

My family suffered also as my children had little time with me. On one occasion my daughter asked to see my Day-Timer appointment book so she could put her name down for some time with me. That caught me by surprise and actually helped start me on the road to find a way out of the movement.

At the time I was told by those over me I had to go back to school. This was a directive the Lord sovereignly told me not to follow. I was also told I would not be allowed to minister in any meetings because I was fat. Unless I lost weight and went back to school I would be replaced. I was also instructed to control my wife as she spoke out of turn and had opinions that were counter to what the male leadership was saying. Women were also confined to female roles, though nobody knew exactly what that meant. As a result I began to see how the body of Christ would be hindered by losing out on the giftedness of the women in our fellowship. These incidents and many similar events finally led to my leaving the movement. When I did leave, at the next meeting of those who were in leadership over me, it was prophesied that I would die in six months because of my arrogance, disobedience, and unwillingness to submit to authority. I lived anxiously for the next six months, and finally broke free from that fear 7 or 8 months later.

Retrospectively speaking, as a friend once said, the Lord deals with us in the kindest way possible. Barbara and I learned things we will never forget. We learned that true authority comes from God alone and Jesus is well able to shepherd his sheep. We can now smell controlling and manipulating authority a mile away. We also treat our brethren with dignity, humility and above all, love. We never try to "fix" people; we leave that up to the Lord. I still believe in the Ephesians 4 truths concerning the need for apostles, prophets, evangelists, pastors and teachers, for the equipping of the saints.

But the way it is to be done was never to be the way we saw and practiced it. True authority enables godly leadership, both male and female, to support and lift up one another in gentleness, humility, and love. As Paul states in Galatians 3:28, "There is neither Jew nor Greek, there is neither slave nor free man, there is neither male or female, for you are all one in Christ." The church over the years has lost immeasurable gifts by not employing men and women in all the callings of God. It is through these kinds of experiences we learned anew that God truly does cause all things to work together for good.

Chapter 30

BREAD OF LIFE

BREAD OF LIFE is the teaching ministry that grew out of my radio program at KORU. The teaching opportunities started coming in the Fall of 1968. A woman who had heard me on the radio asked if I would teach a Bible study in her home. The Lord gave me the green light so I decided to give it a try. Within several months I was speaking at four meetings a week and by the Spring of 1969 we had eight meetings going on. I would do my radio program in the morning and then have a 1:30 PM teaching meeting and later in the day an evening meeting.

The meetings grew so fast that by 1970 we had incorporated Bread of Life as a ministry unto itself. The ministry demands on me were heavy enough by 1971 that we knew it was time to leave ORU and KORU. After the aforementioned meetings with Oral Roberts, I left ORU with his blessing. I went full time into the teaching ministry. At that time I had between 12-15 home meetings a week in Tulsa and on the weekends traveled all over Oklahoma, Arkansas, Texas, Louisiana, and Kansas.

It was clear to Barbara and me that God's hand was on those meetings. All sorts of miracles took place including sovereign salvations and healings as well as dramatic deliverances. The first month after leaving KORU we were concerned that we would have enough money to provide for our family. We had received a wicker basket full of fruit for Christmas the year before. We decided to put that basket on our dresser and we asked the Lord for provision. We turned our support wholly over to Him as He had instructed me never to directly ask for support.

As the first month rolled by, various people would give us money. I would take that money and put it into the basket. By the end of the month I figured there might be two to three hundred dollars in there. To my surprise, when I added up what we had put in there, the amount was more than my salary had been at ORU. Barbara and I were astounded as we believed God had quite literally multiplied the money. To this day, over forty years later, we have never asked for support but God has superabundantly met our every need.

There was no doubt in our minds of God's leading in all of the meetings but my busy schedule also meant I was gone from home a lot. This put a heavy load on Barbara. As we talked about that together, I suggested perhaps I should pull back some so I could be a bigger help to her. Barbara responded very strongly and with obvious clarity from the Lord, by saying, "Tom, don't ever use the kids and me as an excuse not to obey God". Her heart and the Lord's will came through loud and clear. This was never a concern again.

Despite the rapid growth of the ministry, we had no intention of forming a church. Instead we encouraged many who came to the Lord to attend existing churches. However when the Shepherding movement began, many began looking to us as their church. To accommodate them we made a decision to host a meeting for them in our home. This continued on until the time we left the Shepherding movement in 1979.

When I left the movement, most of the people left the Bread of Life fellowship. The damage caused to us and those around us through that movement took some time to heal. I needed a way to provide for my family during that difficult time. We decided to begin a cleaning service that we called Marturion. We serviced all kinds of offices and business establishments. We had several young men and women who were living with us at the time. They joined my children and me in the business. This became our means of support for the next few years.

In the midst of all this my father and mother had permanently moved to Tulsa in 1978. My father had been diagnosed with terminal prostate cancer. To make things more complicated, my parents had been caring for his older cousin, Clara, for over a year. With my Dad's illness, they would no longer be able to care for her. So in 1979 we remodeled our home and moved my father and mother, along with Clara, into our home. By this time all eight or so of the young men and woman who had lived with us for five or six years were married or in school or jobs. In the Lord's timing that opened up space for our new house guests.

In 1979 we met with my father's doctor who told us we must put my dad in a 24 hour care facility. As we had asked the Lord about this, I informed the doctor that we were going to take care of him in our home. The doctor was visibly angry with our response. He told us that was foolish and impossible. I answered that the only question he had to answer was whether or not he would help us or should we find another doctor. He fumed and dismissed us so we found a local Hospice service who would help us at home. Looking back, the experience both for my father and our children was priceless. For example, my youngest daughter, Sarah, would go in and talk and sing to my Dad every day even though she was only three years old. When Dad died in 1980 she couldn't understand why we were sad. She said that Grandpa had told her he was going to be with Jesus very soon and that she should be very happy with him. She was. And, in light of her words, so were we.

As for the young people who lived with us periodically, I rejoice to say that the relationships we formed with them over the years remain as strong as ever. One young man named Jimmy, his wife and family are in Arizona where he is the Rector of a large Episcopal church. Another one, Gerald and his wife and family, live in Kansas City where he retired as a judge after 25+ years. A third couple, Bruce and Debbie, stayed in Tulsa for many years where he became our first elder and teacher. There are many more I could name but suffice it to say, true, non-authoritarian, discipleship happened in our midst by the grace of God.

During the middle 1970's Bread of Life decided to start our own school. Our practice was to home-school the children until the 7th grade and then have school based classes for them until the 12th grade. Many graduated from our school while others finished in public schools. At first the classes met in homes with parents teaching using whatever curriculum we could find in those years. During the 70s, 80s, and early 90s, the school went on to meet in many places including rented buildings, public schools, a Presbyterian church, and an Episcopal church. When we tested the students on the State tests we found they tested usually at least three grades higher than the public schools. We learned that one of the reasons for our success was that teachers and students were never in adversarial roles. The whole school was family.

The school ran beautifully for many years into the late 1990s. By that time we felt the anointing to continue had left. Rather than try and push on without the Lord's clear presence, we felt it better to bring the school to a close. The memories are endless and filled with great joy. We learned in the process that unless a positive and mutually experienced vision motivates a group of people, just as in government, a bureaucratic attitude can come in and perpetuate something that, having served its purpose, should be lovingly put to sleep.

In 1981 Barbara and I went to Israel. We brought my mother with us. They stayed for two weeks while I, my friend Dr. Farah and his wife Joanne, and Jim, a dear brother in the Lord, stayed another five weeks. We shared the good news of Jesus in kibbutzim from southern Israel up to the Lebanon border. Our daughter Rebecca had been in Israel for almost a year along with a young lady named Brenda who had lived with us for some time. Those five weeks really healed me from some deep hurts and cynicism that had crept in during the Shepherding years.

In 1981 Bread of Life Fellowship started to grow again. We kept meeting in our home on Saturday nights and the freedom, worship, and prayer flowed like living water. In the mid 1980's I was introduced to Gene Edwards and attended some prayer gatherings in Maine that he held. Through that connection I got to know Lance and Christie Thollander, beginning a relationship we cherish deeply to this day. Lance would later invite me to be on the board for Hope Builders International, on which I have served for many years. Barb and I were also invited to participate as part of the ministry team at two Forge Summer programs organized by Hope Builders where young leaders from around the world gathered for month long training and fellowship sessions in Charlottesville, VA. That has been a life giving experience for all involved.

Chapter 31

STANDING FIRM TO THE END

As A RESULT of the Shepherding movement and some events that took place in the Tulsa area in the mid 1980's, I was on the receiving end of many personal attacks. My reputation was maligned by those who disagreed with me or had heard and believed things that were not true. As a result we experienced a great deal of rejection from many we thought were our friends. Nonetheless we learned that we should not try to defend or explain ourselves. It turns out that many of God's people, just like people in the world, seem to have an insatiable appetite for gossip and back biting. This is nothing new. As Paul wrote to the Galatians, *"If you bite and devour one another, take care that you do not consume one another."* As a result many rumors circulated about us for several years that had no basis whatever in reality.

God, in His faithfulness, turned us inward in a healthy way. Bread of Life as a fellowship was healthy and growing. Family, fellowship and school brought us together to truly experience life in the body of Christ in a way we never could have otherwise. We initially were concerned that this inward turning would be unhealthy and it could have been without the daily leading of the inner voice, the Holy Spirit. As a fellowship we experienced a type of communal hearing that also included the children. The fruit was a joyful freedom that was free from religious influences. We discovered the body of Christ could truly be led by its head Jesus. I recall one of the sisters involved in the school team would receive leadings concerning how to group the students, how to put different ages together, and very successfully teach them. We teased her about these leadings, but the fruit was apparent.

Family life in our home was full and stretching. Dad died in 1980 whereas my mother lived until 2000 to the age of 97. I teased her that she was older than Oklahoma which became a state in 1907. Clara, my Dad's cousin, preceded her in death by two years. So having two elderly people with us along with school and family, life was busy. I feel these last years, although much smaller and more hidden than some of our earlier ministry years, have been packed with great and holy experiences. An example of that is the students I had the privilege of teaching during those years and the relationships with them that have lasted as they have grown into fine men and women who love Jesus wholeheartedly.

To have had daily opportunities to teach and influence through relationship has been a great personal blessing and has produced lasting fruit. That is also why when the anointing that had been on the school for many years dimmed and an attitude of preservation began to set in, the Lord lovingly helped us put the school to sleep. Again as is often true in government and business, such ventures begin with clarity and dynamic joy, nevertheless, over time they can become something man feels he needs to perpetuate at all costs. This has happened all too often in the church and its structures producing a malaise that kills the life and preserves the shell even when the life is gone.

During those years we continued to have many unusual opportunities to serve the Lord's people. On one occasion Barb and I were at home teaching our fellowship kids when we heard a knock at the door. When we opened the door we were faced with a young girl who was selling Bibles. It was a typical very hot Tulsa day so I invited her in for something to drink. When I innocently asked her how things were going, she burst into tears. She poured out how she had taken the job in rebellion and had been deceived concerning the integrity of her employers. She was living in fear as they threatened her with unhappy consequences should she not meet their expectations.

After an hour of talking with her, Barb and I felt we ought to open our home to her and see what God might do. We invited her to come and live with us until she could find out what she should do. Without hesitation she took us up on our offer. She left and got the few possessions she had and moved in that night. Over the next few days as we probed deeper into her story, some of her poor decision making came into the light. On the one hand, she began to see how truly disrespectful and rebellious she had been to her parents. Still, she felt guilty and was afraid to even try to go home. She had been raised in a strong, God fearing family and felt she was truly living the life of a prodigal.

After a week of listening to her and just loving her, she began to wonder if her Dad and Mom would let her come home. She was from Chicago. We chose not to press her or demand much from her except that she make herself at home in our family and participate in family life. Within three weeks time she fit right in and became a very joyful young woman. Shortly thereafter she began to long for home. Still feeling afraid of being rejected by her family for running away and realizing that they had no idea where she was, she cautiously asked our advice. We prayed asking the Lord how to proceed.

It seemed right to all of us that I could, with her permission, telephone her Dad and find out where they were at in relation to their daughter. She gave me their number and I called him in Chicago. When I told him who I was and that his daughter was well and living with us in Tulsa, he burst into tears. He sputtered thanksgiving to God that she was safe. He then asked how she ended up with us. I told him the story of her coming and asked if he would like to speak with her. He loudly said "Yes Please!" I handed the phone to his daughter and left the room. They talked for many minutes. All we could tell was that their conversation was punctuated with lots of crying and asking for forgiveness. That came from both sides. Both father and daughter realized they had had a part in the breakdown of their relationship.

As their conversation wound down, she called me back into the room and asked if I would talk with her father. I got on the phone and told him I would put his daughter on a plane to Chicago the next day. Two days later we received a call from the young girl. She was filled with gratitude to us, her family and to God. I heard from the father a couple of days later. He also was filled with love and gratitude to have his daughter home.

Also during this period of school, family, fellowship, I was invited to start a Bible study by some friends. That was in 1982 and that meeting still continues on Tuesday mornings to this day, over thirty years later. These friends, who have become old geezers like me, have been a blessing beyond belief. We have shared so many experiences life has to offer, including diseases like Alzheimer's, suffering, deep disappointments, and the like, and have watched as the Lord has met each of us in unique and miraculous ways. They have sustained me and taught me that growing older and feebler is not a threat but an opportunity to show more and more of the grace of God.

These brethren have faced deep physical pain with grace and joy. Some have suffered the loss of just about everything and have come through with rich testimonies of God's grace and strength. Over these decades of fellowship, teaching, prayer and revelation for specific situations I have witnessed the faithfulness of God. He is God whether we find ourselves in retirement homes, Alzheimer units, mental clinics, and even going through family rejection. I have seen sacrifice and love like never before by families of some of my older friends. People like these encourage me to "die with my boots on," carrying forward the message of God's kingdom of love, and not simply protecting my earthly possessions. My prayer for us all is that the Lord will allow us to stand firm in Him, living out our lives to His glory.

Appendix

LIFE LESSONS

1. Why Walking by Faith is so Important

2. The Well Placed Lie

3. The Nicolaitan Heresy

4. How Institutional Religion Can Stand in the Way of Spiritual Growth

5. Not the Report I Wanted

6. The Value of an Old Geezer

7. The Keeper and the Kept

8. Significant Dreams

9. What Does Healthy Discipleship Look Like?

10. Four Experiences God Uses to Change Lives

1. Why Walking by Faith is so Important

There are many scriptures that urge us to walk by faith. Two of them are 1 Corinthians 5:7, which says, "for we walk by faith not by sight," and Ephesians 2:8, which says, "For by grace you have been saved through faith; and that is not yourselves, it is the gift of God. " Another clear example of being encouraged to live lives of faith is seen in Hebrews 11, the New Testament chapter that chronicles Old Testament believers who walked by faith. Here is an experience concerning faith that happened to Barbara and I that forever changed our hearts concerning the walk of faith.

One day while reading Hebrews 11 and marveling at the experiences of those who had walked by faith, verse 8 struck me. This verse states, "By faith Abraham, when he was called, obeyed by going out to a place which he was to receive for an inheritance; and he went out, not knowing where he was going."

I stopped and told Barbara this verse makes absolutely no sense. How can someone not know where he is going? In that moment I sensed the voice in my belly telling me God can only guide us to a place of His calling if we obey by moving. He has given us free will and will not drive us to follow him against our wills. However, if we will move in a direction, He can turn us anywhere as long as we daily choose to obey His voice and move. Even if I misunderstand the voice of God in my belly, if I move forward in the faith I have, He can, will, and does turn me to His calling and destiny. Barbara and I have lived this out hundreds of times.

Over the years in my role as a pastor, many have poured out their hearts to me concerning their calling in the Lord. They want to follow the Lord but are not clear where He is leading them. The problem often is that they are literally frozen, unable and afraid to move in any direction. They do not want to miss

God's will or act presumptuously. Consequently, some have been afraid to do anything out of fear of doing the wrong thing.

My response is to share with them that they have to move, or step out in a direction by faith and trust that God can turn them completely around. He is on their side. He understands the desires of their hearts. If it turns out they are going in the wrong direction, He has the power to change their course to suit His desires. Sadly, too often, the response has been to still be afraid. I have become convinced through these encounters that fear is actually the opposite of faith, not unbelief.

Thankfully, many have made the glad discovery, as Barbara and I have, that God does cause all things to work together for good, even our mistakes and wrong decisions. Our heavenly Father will work these things for good. The result of all this is we can move forward in our lives with a confident trust in our God. The moves we make will allow Him to show us exactly what He wants. God can turn every response of ours for good. And He is good and loving enough to do just that.

2. The Well Placed Lie

The well placed lie is one powerful way the enemy influences the lives of believers that we are too often not aware of. Jesus said that Satan was a liar and a murderer from the beginning. In every lie is the potential of death, unless truth enters and changes its destiny. The kind of death I am talking about here can involve the death of a relationship, estrangement between family members, the dissolution of a business practice and so on.

I had a friend who told me that you become like whatever you give yourself to. I have thought of that over the years and have found it to be true, even if what you have given yourself to is a lie. I have also seen that the longer a lie goes unchallenged, the more difficult it can be to uproot and replace with truth. Many times the lie becomes so deeply imbedded in a person's life that it is virtually impossible to dislodge without a God given revelation. The Spirit of the One who is Truth Incarnate can, and will, lovingly reveal lies that we have taken into our life fabric. In His timing they can be brought to the surface and the Lord can then deliver the person from the lie's tyranny.

One song that illustrated how lies can be developed in us was "You've got To Be Carefully Taught" from the musical South Pacific. That song contained these revealing words,

> "You've got to be taught to hate and fear,
> You've got to be taught from year to year
> It's got to be drummed in your dear little ear
> You've got to be carefully taught
>
> You've got to be taught to be afraid
> Of people whose eyes are oddly made
> And people whose skin is a different shade
> You've got to be carefully taught.
>
> You've got to be taught before it's too late
> Before you are six or seven or eight
> To hate all the people your relatives hate.
> You've got to be carefully taught."

Well placed lies, like those referred to in this song, can affect or infect a life, family, business, school, government, legal system, all sorts of relationships, and indeed, a whole culture. To the contrary, it's also just as true that a well placed truth can affect all of the above for the positive.

The well placed lie found its first home in the garden. The enemy deceived men and women into thinking they would be better off to be like God, knowing good and evil, rather than living by God himself as their life. This deception led to separation from God and the establishing of what to me is religious behavior. By that I mean man trying to reach and please God through establishing systems of worship based on man's behavior rather than living in the safety and blessedness of what God has accomplished for us in Christ. The problem with this is that man ends up in the driver's seat using God or gods in order to implement his ends. This can play out in every aspect of life, including government. Religion has many times been used by governments to control and manipulate those in their power. The converse is also true. Religious movements have taken over the reins of government to establish control of the masses.

On a personal level, here is an example of how a well placed lie can affect a man's relationship with God in an unhealthy way. I know a man who for much of his life as a believer, teacher, and pastor, found it difficult to receive praise. If someone would say "well done," the compliment would often produce guilt and self-judgment. Thoughts would come like, "I must be a self centered deceiver, an arrogant and self-promoting man." This man fought these feelings for much of his adult life. They produced shame, unworthiness and internal disclaimers like, "Well, they don't know the real me."

To quote author Gary Barkalow, "The counterfeit of humility is shame, which is often misunderstood and accepted as humility. Shame is the painful feeling, valid or invalid, of unworthiness, disgrace, or contempt. These feelings of shame can create very similar appearing behaviors externally as humility does. But the effect of shame is the belief that "I am nothing and have nothing to offer," causing a person to rarely exert him or herself or take risks and always offer disclaimers or apologies when sharing with others."

The man in question, along with his wife, was on his way to a meeting of believers in Christ that was to start the next day. He was to be one of the speakers at the meeting. On the way he fell under strong feelings of anger, fear, shame, and self-loathing. The feelings were so powerful he wanted to return home and not attend the meeting. Still they journeyed on to their destination. In the early morning hours, unable to sleep, he got up and gave vent to all of the above feelings. He was mad at God, his wife, and himself, but ultimately blamed himself for the feelings. Thoughts like, "What the hell was he doing going to a meeting where there were "real" men and women of God present, and not this shameful arrogant unworthy phony. Why had he even been asked?"

At about three in the morning his wife woke up. She wondered what was going on as her husband's despair was evident. When he told her what was going on, she tried to inject some truth into his thinking. He quickly rejected her suggestions and told her they ought to just pack up and go home. In the middle of this emotional swamp, the wife began to pray for her husband, asking God to break through with the truth about this man. Something wonderful began to happen.

The man immediately saw himself as a little boy of around 7 or 8 years old. He was coming home from grammar school singing at the top of his lungs. Later that evening his parents called him into the front room. They told him that the neighbors had heard him singing and they had been embarrassed by the song that he was blasting out. They in turn also felt embarrassed and told him to stop singing like that in public. The message to the boy was clear, "You're an embarrassment and showoff, don't ever do that again."

The lie that he was an embarrassment was planted deep in the boy's heart. From that point on, whenever he did anything well like get a hit in baseball, sing a solo in church, or win a race, he was always cautioned not to get proud or embarrass his parents or himself. In the motel that night this older man saw clearly how the lie that he was a perpetual embarrassment had been planted in his life, even if unwittingly, by what had been said to him. In that moment he forgave his parents, and allowed the power of the Spirit of Truth to free him from the lie. He wasn't an embarrassment! He did have eternal value before his heavenly Father and to those around him.

The result of that freeing revelation continues to this day. This man was now able without shame or pride to receive the kind remarks of others and to enjoy himself in Christ. He went on to the meeting the next day where he was astounded at the freedom he experienced and the love he felt for God, himself and others. It was like being born again, all over again.

How do I know this story to be true? I am that man.

As we continue to look at the power of lies in other fields an important side note is needed. Lies, like the weeds that grew alongside the good seed in the parable of the Kingdom in Matthew 13, grow along with the good seed. In the parable the people are told to let the weeds grow as we don't know how to pull them without also pulling up some of the good planting. The fact is that only the Lord can show us what the truth is about us. He knows what lies we can deal with and what lies we are unable to deal with. We need His help to sort out what is true about us and what messages need to be abandoned and left behind.

A beautiful example of this is found in the story *The Voyage of the Dawn Treader* by C.S. Lewis. In the story a mean and somewhat despicable boy named Eustace gets turned into a dragon through his love for riches. This experience completely changes his outlook on life. Eventually Aslan, the great Lion, a picture of Christ in the story, comes to Eustace's aid and directs him to peel off the dragon skin so that he can return to his real self. Eustace tries over and over to peel off his skin, only to find another layer underneath. Finally, in his despair he calls out to Aslan to help him. The great lion then lets Eustace know that he cannot peel off that dragon nature by himself. Aslan must do it for him. So with much pain, Aslan tears deep into Eustace's skin and finally peels off his false covering. Eustace begins to walk in a new freedom and peace he had never known before. As Aslan was for Eustace, Jesus is the master pruner in our lives. He will show us what needs to be done so that we can walk in the glorious truth of who we are in Him.

As we look to the Lord about this He may show us that some lies need prayer and fasting to be fully dealt with, while others need only to be confronted to be overcome. It is also true that many of the well placed lies in the life of a believer can only be dealt with in true community. We need our brothers and sisters to communicate the power and love of God to us. In his marvelous book, *Life Together*, Dietrich Bonheoffer, writes concerning Christian community, "Sin demands to have a man by himself. It withdraws him from community. It shuns the light." In other words, sin demands that any person with the fruit of a lie or other sin in their life, go it alone in false humility. As I was helped by my wife's prayers to break through the debilitating messages I had believed to be true, we help one another to work through the wrong headed lies that we have been told either by the enemy, ourselves, those around us or our culture at large.

Going along with this, half-truths concerning the gospel must be examined and replaced with the whole gospel that Jesus preached. That gospel is the Gospel of the Kingdom of God. Too many of us have been handed and have also handed on, half truths about what God wants. Partial gospels, like the Baptism of the Holy Spirit, Healing, and Deliverance, do not show us the full measure of God's heart and plan. While they all contain some truth, they cannot deliver the fullness of God to us. That message and fullness is found in His Kingdom. All these other things find their proper place within that. The kingdom message is like a seed but the great difference is that it never ceases to grow. God's Kingdom is eternal. When we settle for a half gospel, we are inevitably disappointed. This explains why so many brethren drop out of following Christ after experiencing disappointment with what they have found in church relationships. The Kingdom never ceases to grow whereas the lesser truncated gospels wear out and exhaust us. May the Lord continue to lead us all into the wonderful Truth regarding Himself, who we are in Him and his Kingdom purposes for us.

3. The Nicolaitan Heresy

Many years ago I was reading in the book of Revelation about the Nicolaitan teaching that was hated by the Lord in two of the seven churches, Ephesus and Pergamum. As I pondered just what the heresy or teaching was that the Lord hated, I started to journey through all of my reference material. The subject was on my mind for weeks as I continued my research.

Most of the commentators supposed that the teaching may have come from Nicolas who was one of the seven in Acts 6, who were appointed to serve the Greek and Jewish widows. However, as I studied and researched this subject I grew more and more dissatisfied with the commentaries and research. For instance, the name Nicolaitans, according to the early church fathers (Ignatius , Irenaeus, Clement of Alexandria, Tertullian, Hippolytus) refers to those who, while professing themselves to be Christians, lived licentiously.

As I pondered all the research I grew even more troubled. At about this same time in the early 80's I was reading some of E. Stanley Jones writings from the early 1920's. He wrote in Acts 6 about how the apostles felt they should not serve tables and that others of sound reputation and Spirit should be appointed so they could center on prayer and ministry of the word. Jones postulated that this was a grievous error that caused a problem that even today infects and affects the church and true church life; that being the division between the clergy and the laity that inevitably creates first and second class Christians. Jones felt strongly that this action in Acts 6 created problems the church has never recovered from. I could not help but be moved by his insight and that led me to further study.

I eventually stumbled across the Greek word Nicolaitan in a concordance. I read that the word came from two other words, nikao, meaning "to conquer," and laos, meaning "the people", or "laity." There is no ancient authority for a sect of the Nicolaitans from which the word was derived. All of a sudden

I sensed a great personal relief. I had always believed that Jesus' sacrifice on the cross had done away with all distinctions between people. An example of that is seen in Matthew 23:8 where Jesus told his disciples, "But do not be called Rabbi; for One is your teacher, and you are all brothers."

I realized that Jesus was eliminating forever the divided clergy and lay distinction and creating an equal brotherhood. Eugene Peterson's translation of Matt 23:8 in The Message, puts it this way, "Don't let people do that to you, put you on a pedestal like that. You all have a single teacher, and you are all classmates. Don't set up people as experts over your life, letting them tell you what to do." As a result I felt understanding flow into me about the heresy the Lord hated in the book of The Revelation of Jesus Christ. Basically it is a two tiered understanding and practice of how life in the body of Christ should be organized with a professional clergy giving directions and a non-professional laity following them.

The basic assumption is that God gives "the clergy" and all the laity need to do is obey and follow. This two-tiered system supposedly came into existence after Jesus' resurrection and the giving of the Holy Spirit. One example of that is found in Acts 6 when the twelve can't serve the common folk and must give their time to minister the word of God. They needed to be released from mundane duties so they could do the more important work of ministry. In my view, however, this attitude was not in Jesus who could wash the disciples' feet as well as teach and preach.

The sad fact is that even after Pentecost the old system of priest and laity still existed in the practice of the New Testament church. Old patterns die hard. It is insightful to see in Acts 6 that the anointing spread at least to Stephen and perhaps others. Acts 7 ends with Jesus' revelation to Stephen even as he dies. The fact that Stephen could minister to the daily needs of the people and still be a dynamic minister of the Gospel could have been an indication of the New Covenant way of doing things. It is my opinion that while the Jerusalem church needed to be scattered for the sake of spreading the Gospel, it also needed to be dispersed because it was still manifesting Old Testament practices. This is likely one reason that the anointing moved eventually to Antioch where there were also prophets and leaders did not have such strong ties to Old Testament tradition.

I would point out that the gift ministries spoken of by Paul in Ephesians 4:11 were not authority roles but gifts to and for the body of Christ. The leadership our Lord Jesus provided for in the body of Christ was made available so that the body could be led by Jesus through the Holy Spirit. That authority was never meant to be a New Testament hierarchy where authority was derived from an office or title. Rather the authority was placed in the assembling of the body under the Spirit. Through the ages we generally have not really trusted that this could possibly be the case. As a result we have seen the rise of denominationalism, i.e. Orthodoxy, Catholicism, Protestantism, and so on where leadership is centered in the clergy. That idea that God could lead His body through His Spirit and not through hierarchical structures requires a much more active and present God, revealing his grace, power, and wisdom, than the various human centered authority structures that have risen up do.

Most everyone agrees that the church must have leadership. Generally, however, the dominant kind that has been known is the "flow chart" model. In the Shepherding movement it was taught that your place in the body of Christ could only be discovered in one way. You asked the Lord to whom you should submit and then who should submit to you. In that regard Derek Prince once said that though he was not a supporter of the Papal authority system, he would rather be under that than many of the Pentecostal leaders he had known who seemed to have no boundaries or corrective procedures at all. At least the Pope had restraints. Those restraints, all too often, seemed to be lacking in many so called Evangelical associations and ministries who say they answer only to God.

My point is this: true authority and leadership are available to
the body of Christ but were not designed to be two-tiered or
flow-chart oriented. True authority lies in Godly influence that
is never forced but only shared. It seems to come and go like
the wind of the Spirit spoken of by Jesus in John 3. An example
would have been our school. The school operated for 20+years
with an organizational structure that flowed with power, love,
and mutual service. Those in leadership never looked to be
overbearing but humble and open to the mutual seeking of
the Lord. After those years a change began to take place and
the sweetness and flowing love of the Holy Sprit began to be
replaced with the need for much more control and obedience.
Those things had been there all along by the influence of the
Holy Spirit. As the power of the Holy Spirit's authoritative
influence faded, we who had begun in the Spirit did not wish
to end in the flesh. For that reason we allowed the school to
close. This was a very painful decision as we had enjoyed
more than twenty years of being free from religious hierarchy.
Rather than enshrine that hierarchy we let the school go.

I have seen over the years the results of this two-tiered
view of church and church life. No wonder I thought, as Jones
had written, that the harm this has caused the church over
the centuries is huge. May our Lord enable us to repent of
this heresy and return to a truly equal brotherhood where the
service of prayer and ministry of the word is not separated from
table-serving. Jesus could wash feet as well teach and pray as
there was no distinction in Him between secular and sacred.

I first taught on this in the early 1980's among brothers I
knew well. The first public teaching I did on the Nicolaitan
heresy was in 1998 at a Pastoral conference. Afterwards I was
accosted by pastors who said that this teaching would destroy
the church. They were adamant that I should repent. In spite
of that experience, over the past years I have only grown more
and more convinced that the church needs to be set free from

ministerial hierarchy. Connected with a hierarchical view of how the body of Christ should be organized has been a corresponding devaluation of the place of women in the body. That being the case, along with a better understanding of how to combat the Nicolaitan heresy, we also need a revolution regarding the role of women in the body of Christ. Overt male dominance under the guise of exercising church authority has crippled the church and deprived it of many gifts. As the founder of the Salvation Army William Booth wrote, "Some of my best men are women." Amen and Amen!

4. How Institutional Religion Can Stand in the Way of Spiritual Growth

Over the years I have seen time and time again how institutional religion woefully prepares young men and women for true ministry. It's as though the dispensers of religious information believe that simply providing knowledge of God can touch and bring healing to the broken hearted of this world. But knowledge in and of itself is not enough. People need to have an encounter with the living God himself.

Information and knowledge about God and his institutions may provide a modicum of salve for the seeking soul, but like a wound that heals on the surface, it leaves a deep unhealed wound. Jesus always heals from the inside out. We have to have real knowledge of Him in our hearts, not just teaching about him that fills our brains. But, sadly, superficiality seems to be the stock and trade of religion and its institutions. The lie goes like this, "If I understand and know things in my mind, they are therefore reality in my life. " Nothing could be further from the truth or more subtly evil.

Sooner or later both the minister and the ministered, come to a mutual lie where they pretend that as long as things look good on the outside, they will not deal with what is really going on within them. Chaos, fear, and doubt may be alive and well in a person's heart but they are pressed down because they are not supposed to be present in a believer's life. The Christian life becomes a morality play of sorts where we allow outward appearances to define who we are rather than the depth of our relationship with the Lord Jesus. It's similar to the story entitled, "The Emperor Has No Clothes." Sooner or later those in the play often become tired of maintaining the image and move away from vibrant faith and other believers because they simply don't know how be more real.

As this plays out, neither clergy nor laity comes face to face with the reality that there is no "Immanuel" in the picture, that is, a God who is truly with us. We are on our own. What could have been vital faith with an Immanent God moving in and through lives becomes a kind of phony cultural morality. The posing that results disguises and becomes a replacement for the God who "IS." This type of religious living also never really challenges the culture that it lives in the midst of. It presents God as a benign old man who has no real power to do anything. We pat the old guy (God) on the shoulder but give him no real recognition, as we all know he either doesn't exist or he's not really interested in what's going on with us.

When someone really does meet the true and living God, he often is deemed by the religious institutions as delusional. In my case, for example, when I shared with my superiors my experiences with the Spirit of God, my District Superintendent told me that what I needed was a good dose of Pepto Bismol. He said that would take care of those tongues. Sadly, real faith experiences like the ones I had, can present a challenge to religion, its need to have all the answers, and the self-perpetuation of its cause by denying those experiences which do not fit within its religious parameters.

I have a life-long friend named Jim who was a rector in the Episcopalian Church. Jim and his wife Mallory influenced and blessed my life for decades. Through the way they were treated I saw the worst side of how ecclesiastical authority can be turned to abuse. The Episcopalian Bishop's treatment of this godly man and his family was atrocious. If ever I had wanted a present-day example of what the Pharisees and Sadducees, plus the Sanhedrin, must have been like in Jesus' day, I had one. As Jesus threatened the religiosity of his day, so Jim and Mallory's lives and ministry threatened the ecclesiastical hierarchy of the Episcopal Church. Sadly the church did not seem to believe in much except to preserve itself and its authority. Jim was literally shut out of the priesthood because he believed the Scripture was inspired and that Jesus could still do today what He had always done. I had a similar experience in the Methodist Church so I could relate.

Jim was ridiculed and stigmatized simply because he was a humble priest of God. It was through Jim's experiences as well as those of dozens of ministers, priests, rabbis, pastors, and many godly laymen I met over the years, that I finally came to realize that one of the greatest enemies of the Christian faith has been religion and religious figures. I saw that the church as an institution likes its saints dead, because, alive, they are too much of a problem. Church history is replete with examples of preserving the institution by human endeavor, i.e. political maneuvering and the strength of natural gifts and strong personalities, rather than the church existing and continuing by the direct operation of the Holy Spirit and the grace of God.

I find instances of this both in Scripture and in Church history. When Moses came down from the mountain with the Ten Commandments, he found the people had constructed a golden calf in his absence. What caused that? Humanity has always wanted a god in its own image. They have a god they can control. When Elijah faced the prophets of Baal, they had done everything from cutting themselves to endlessly crying out for their God to bring fire. What religion loves to do is create a system wherein God is offered man's best intentions and then must act because of what has been performed by his worshippers.

Jesus faced this when he entered the temple and witnessed

what the covenant people had done with the temple worship. They were keeping the outward acts of sacrifice but had long ago left the God they supposedly worshipped. Jesus immediately saw the hypocrisy and challenged it. He overturned the tables and drove out the vendors who made a living off of their religious wares. In the first century city of Ephesus, in a story recorded in the book of Acts, the silversmiths were furious with Paul because his preaching cut deeply into their religious business.

Over the years I slowly learned that the spirit of religion and tradition can also be present in small groups of people. It doesn't take a denomination or a big para-church ministry to have this problem. The reality is that the capacity to become religious in our Christian practice is part of the human condition. Our own ministry also fell into a hypercritical and self-protective mode. We, even in our smallness, had institutionalized ways of thinking and behaving that we then came to expect from those who were part of our fellowship. The outward form of what we were doing came to be more important than the inward reality of knowing Jesus in our lives.

Another equally deceitful thought and expression we had was "Big is bad; small is good." This represented the view that any large ministry, whether local, national, or international, must be bad. Only small ministries were good. Of course, as a small ministry ourselves, that fit perfectly into our world view. Sadly, throughout my years in ministry, I experienced manipulation, threats and the absolute tyranny of so-called and self-proclaimed authorities, both in small circles and large, witnessing first-hand the harm they worked on the people of God.

What is the upshot of all this. A relationship with Christ that is based in who he is in Reality today, and not simply based just on the teachings and the institutions that follow in his wake, often seems to be an inevitable casualty of Christianity as it moves to formalize its practices.

5. Not the Report I Wanted!

Many of us receive news we aren't happy with. The news may concern business relationships, medical issues, church relationships or practices, world events, and problems that arise within our families or circle of friends. Not long ago I received a medical report concerning the return of cancer in my body. The result was that I would be re-doing a procedure that I had undergone several years previously. I write about this because this time around I found a whole new response working in me that I would like to share with you.

The last time I was diagnosed with this cancer, the procedure to deal with it was new to me. As a result I experienced a lot of anxiety. The Lord graciously led me through it and I was cancer free for almost two years. But then the cancer returned. Thankfully, in the interim and before the recent checkup, I had a marvelous revelation that helped me put everything that was happening to me in a new light.

When I received the latest news, I recalled a recent encounter with the Lord. This encounter gave me new insight to an oft quoted verse, a verse I thought I had always understood. The verse is a well known one: Romans 8:28. *"And we know God causes all things to work together for good to those who love God, to those who are called according to His purpose."* (New American Standard Bible) Many times in my walk with Jesus I have quoted and thought I understood and believed this verse. But as I discussed this verse with a friend, he casually mentioned his being struck by the word "causes." As he shared his thoughts with me my insides seemed to open up, and I realized something brand new and exciting.

Let me state as strongly as possible that I do not believe God causes all things. Rather, I believe that He causes all things to work together for good. God did not cause my cancer, just like He does not cause the hard circumstances or the suffering that comes to many believers. Likewise, things like broken relationships or persecution are not caused by God. These come as a result of living in a fallen world. Our challenge, as Kingdom men and women, is to follow James' New Testament exhortation *"to count it all joy."* (James 1: 2-4. NASB.)

God didn't cause Adam and Eve to eat from the tree of good and evil, Satan did. But God has caused even that to work for good. This may be obvious to you, but what eluded me was that whatever circumstance I am in, whether good or bad, I can truly know that God can and will cause it to work for good. By good or bad I do not mean eating out of the tree of good and evil, but rather drawing my life out of the Tree of Life, and letting the good or bad, right or wrong, stay in God's hands.

When my life is in God's hands, the good and bad are all subject to Him. If I am the one determining what is good or bad, I disallow the Lord the opportunity to cause the events that take place to work for good. When I am the one deciding what is good or bad, I will inevitably be disappointed, especially if I don't get what I want the way I wanted it. If I have a pre-determined outcome that is not fulfilled, I end up in despair. Why? Because I have eaten from the wrong tree. I am living on the basis of the knowledge of what I think is good and what I think is bad (evil). The reality is that everything that comes out of the tree of good and evil results in death. Even if the good from that tree seems right for a time, its end result is death.

With all that in mind, before my checkup I had, along with many others, prayed for a good report of no cancer. As I sat waiting for the Doctor I was amazed at how calm I was, knowing that whatever the report was, cancer or no cancer, God would cause it to work for good. When the Doctor gave his report that the cancer may have returned, nothing changed within me. I said inwardly, "Wow, how is God going to cause this to work for good?" I didn't have to work up a positive confession, making sure I quoted the right scriptures. All I had to do was give myself and my life anew to the Lord Jesus. I left the Doctor's office excited to see how He would use this latest development. My simple revelation has been, and continues to be, there is nothing our Lord can't use if we will only give ourselves to Him.

I think I am finally getting it!!!

During that same period of time I also experienced some marvelous times with Jesus that I believe show so much of the Lords wisdom and grace. In the chapter about "Confession is Possession," I referred to what the Lord taught my wife Barbara and I concerning that very presumptuous theology. That theology demanded Jesus to heal as long as we faithfully confessed the scriptures that speak of His healing will and how it was all accomplished at Calvary.

One such text often used is Isaiah 53:4-5 and it is repeated in 1 Peter 2:24. Another often used text is Romans 10: 8-11 that speaks of "confessing" from the heart, as well as a text from James 5:15-18 which speaks of prayer for healing. These texts do encourage us to believe in the Lord Jesus and, as an old mentor Oral Roberts used to say, to "Expect a miracle." The fact is that over the years Barbara and I have seen first hand many wonderful healing miracles. Still, the issue for us has never been a question of God's ability and desire to heal. The issue for us became "our desire" must be "God's desire." But through experience we have found that we as the children of God are not in the position to demand anything from our Lord but rather to trust Him in all things.

I recall a chapel gathering at ORU many years ago when President Oral Roberts spoke to the students, faculty, and staff on what he called "a very important truth." That truth was that God often heals through death! As a healing evangelist whose ministry and University were built on the reality of healing he had to embrace a reality that made some of his followers wince. He continued by saying that he always prayed for healing leaving the results in the hands of the One he trusted in all things. That result was that God had indeed on many occasions used and brought healing through death. At that time Barbara and I had gone through the death of our baby. This insight helped to heal us and enabled us to trust the healing Jesus even more.

Around this same time my dear friend and brother Tommy Tyson, the first chaplain at ORU, reminded us that everyone that Jesus healed eventually died. He even jokingly said that Lazarus would probably answer if threatened with death: "Been there, done that." At the same time a dear friend of 30+ years, Dr. Charles Farah, who taught in ORU's seminary wrote a book entitled, *"From the Pinnacle of the Temple."* In this book he describes how Jesus was tempted by the devil with Scripture. In His temptation after His baptism by John and being in the wilderness for 40 days, the devil tempts Him to work a miracle, i.e. turn stones into bread. Jesus' response is clear and clean, "Man shall not live by bread alone but by every word that proceeds out of the mouth of God." By so doing, Jesus refused to be tempted by legitimate need.

It is the next temptation that the devil used that gave rise to Dr. Farah's book title. The devil takes Him to the pinnacle of the temple and says, "Throw yourself down; for it is written He will give His angels charge concerning you and on their hands they will bear you up lest you strike your foot against a stone." Here the devil used the Scripture for his own demonic purposes. President Roberts and Tommy Tyson encouraged Dr. Farah in the publishing of the book to give opportunity for discussion about healing and the confessional theology named above that was causing so much concern in those days.

Many dear brethren were deeply wounded by being accused of unbelief because they didn't quote the right texts long enough or with not enough faith. As a result they weren't healed and had failed God. I recall a seminar at ORU where

I had the privilege along with Dr. Farah and many others of debating this theology. The debate's outcome was healthy and many people were set free from condemnation they had experienced when told they just didn't have enough faith or they didn't believe the scripture or they didn't "confess" the right scriptures. These and many other experiences with healing, miracles, and even a resurrection from the dead taught us to never underestimate the power of God in the land of the living but to leave the outcomes to him.

This brings me back to not getting the report I wanted. While I was undergoing treatment for bladder cancer I had a round of therapy that was exceedingly painful. During that time I was sitting on the side of my bed in excruciating pain and I cried out to the Lord Jesus for healing. I confessed every healing text I knew and the pain didn't leave. In tears I continued crying out that this would a marvelous time for a healing. I prayed; "Lord, I believe, help my unbelief." It was in the middle of this that I heard the "voice in the belly" say clearly, "Ask Me!" I said, "Ask you what?" He said, "to bear it with you." I did and He did. Although the pain didn't really subside for about three days, He shared my pain and I experienced a little about the pain He bore and will bear for and with us forever.

The result of that experience has really increased my faith and prayers for healing of all kinds. I continue to find the greatness and the infinite wisdom of our God who revealed himself in the person of the man Jesus, the firstborn of a whole new species. One day when I see Him I will be like Him. I John 3: 1-3 reads, "See how great a love the Father has bestowed upon us, that we should be called children of God; and such we are. For this reason the world does not know us, because it did not know him. Beloved now we are children of God, and it has not appeared as yet what we shall be. We know that when He appears, we shall be like Him, because we shall see Him just as He is. And everyone who has this hope fixed on Him purifies himself, just as He is pure." Thank you Jesus!

6. The Value of an Old Geezer

Out of the blue my grandson asked, "Papa what's an old geezer?

My answer to him was simple, "Someone who has lived quite awhile and has learned a few things."

Then he said, "Boy, Papa, you must have learned a lot of stuff, as old as you are."

This exchange caused me to think about some of the life lessons I have learned. But, perhaps more importantly, the exchange also pushed me to ask of myself if I was still learning new stuff. Was I still experiencing newness of life, or had I fallen into an "old geezer" rut that assumed most of my life was over. Had I reached a stage in life where I was now simply preparing for eternity; where I should allow my life to wind down and prepare my bucket list, hoping I would have time to complete it? Having done so, I would gracefully die?

As this rather pathetic scenario came to mind I remembered a scripture. *"If we have hoped in Christ in this life only, we are of all men to be pitied"* (1 Corinthians 15:19. NASB). In this section the apostle had been talking about baptism and resurrection which he insists must be at the center of our lives. His emphasis was that we must be about Kingdom business daily and that believers already have eternity in their hearts. As a result there is no retirement, no old geezer rut to fall into. I don't necessarily mean there's more to do, but rather that there's more to be. If there's anything older men and women have to offer to those around them it could be stated this way, "Brethren, growing older is a precious and holy gift our Lord has given us, use the life lessons gained to be a blessing to others."

I had a wonderful friend that was called, along with his five brothers, to come home to see their ailing father. When they had all gathered, the father, a farmer with little formal education but a man of great faith, said to them all, "I've called you here to rejoice with me in my home going."

My friend said he never forgot his father's marvelous gift and hoped he would leave the same wonderful gift to his family when he went home to glory. I'm not saying that being an old geezer is living to prepare for death, but that rather a life of faith has great power and glory. This glory, when properly nurtured, can bring life and blessing to many. When they will receive humbly and gratefully their glory and weightiness, so called old geezers can bring a godly, healthy hope to aging.

Modern day society looks increasingly upon old geezers as those whom society should pat on the head while wiping away their drool. Having cared for my parents and my father's cousin in their old age, I am not unaware of the difficulties such care can bring. My wife and her sister also cared for their mother in her final years. But I am also aware of the great opportunities old age presents. As followers of Jesus and representatives of His Kingdom there is no resignation in aging, nor regrets about getting older, but rather an embracing that we are all terminal, something our culture fights to deny. Our society worships youth and does all it can to deny the inevitability of aging, much less actually dying. The biblical "gray head" is often understood as an unfortunate truth we can't avoid. Rarely is going gray described as something to aspire to or esteem.

As I recall my grandson's question, I sense a deep desire to impart to him and my other grandchildren the life lessons I've learned that could be a blessing to their lives. The desire to bless them causes me to be careful about my words, my demeanor, and my relationships with my grandchildren as well as others my life may cross. Jesus warns us about careless words in Matthew 12: 33-37, cautioning us that we will be judged by them. This causes me to gratefully repent of all known and unknown careless words I have not only spoken, but even truthful words spoken outside of the love of Jesus.

Hopefully as we grow into our geezerhood, it will become a time of pouring out and a blessing to all those that our life intersects.

7. The Keeper and the Kept

We are often presented with the idea from our pulpits, our centers of government and our culture in general that we are our brother's keeper. I consider this to be a well placed lie. For years I have heard politicians, educators, and journalists, rabbis and pastors, from liberal to conservative, quote the scriptures and say with authority, "After all, doesn't the Bible teach us that we are our brother's keeper?" This is based on the conversation that Cain had with God when the Lord asked him where Abel was. Of course Cain had killed Abel and knew exactly where he was but did not want to admit to that. So he dodged that question by saying, "How should I know, am I my brother's keeper?" For some reason, despite the fact that God never answered that question, pundits have assumed the correct answer is yes, I am my brother's keeper. I strongly disagree.

It is my strong contention that this lie has perverted religion, culture, government, and law. I contend that Cain's statement was so despicable that God put on him the mark of a liar, a murderer, a wanderer and a vagrant. I believe that God had something infinitely greater in mind for Cain. He could have been a brother or a friend to Abel, but never a keeper or from Abel's perspective, one who is kept. Both are filled with death. All throughout history mankind has perverted this passage in Genesis 4 and foisted upon humankind a caretaker philosophy.

I once heard one of our Presidents say with seemingly indisputable authority that our duty is to be our brother's keeper. His real reason for saying it was simply that he wanted more power centered in the central government as the distributor of social programs and wealth. The fact is that we have all sorts of governments throughout history that have taken this as gospel. Then they have proceeded to collect more power to themselves to put this philosophy into practice. As a result this lie has wounded, destroyed, and ultimately eroded civilizations. Whether it's a benevolent dictator, a despot, or collective type governments like socialism or communism, this philosophy enthrones envy and creates a welfare mentality among those being kept.

I further believe that redistribution of wealth can only be healthy when each individual is in control of their means. The keeper and the kept mentality ultimately destroys human dignity before God and man. The dark reality is that when governments say "Let me keep you," they are also threatening that if you don't, they will destroy you. That generally means the destruction of human dignity, personal responsibility and creative initiative but in the worst cases could mean physical death. This concept of the keeper and the kept also creates class warfare and envy. The fact is that this well placed lie is right now greatly impacting US and European culture to our serious detriment.

8. Significant Dreams

I believe many people can relate to the impact dreams can have on a person's life. The Scripture is full of those to whom God spoke either in dreams or visions. I have had dreams at significant times in my walk with God; three stand out and I remember them with joy and humility.

The first dream came shortly after I became a follower of Jesus and wanted to be a godly father and husband. In the dream I was standing in a long line of men, a line that stretched as far as I could see in both directions. The Lord Jesus was standing before each one of us. Simultaneously He spoke to all of us with these words, "Brothers present to me your wives." In an instant I could see down the lines to the right and the left. Some of the women were clothed in light and looked beautiful. Sadly, many more were battered, bruised, broken and dirty.

Some could not stand up and had to be helped to their feet. Some were weeping loudly, while a few others were laughing and motioning for their husbands to come and dance with them.

In the dream the Lord Jesus was standing directly in front of each of us men. As I looked at His face, I cried out with a loud voice, "Lord Jesus please give me more time!" He looked at me, nodded His head and I immediately woke up. As soon as I awoke, I began to pray, "Lord, help me to love my wife like you love the church because I don't know how!" Over the years I have prayed this prayer many times and the Lord is helping me learn how to love my wife. I trust that a day will come in the future when I can present a beautiful, laughing, dancing bride to my Lord. I long to hear Him say, "Well done!" in this area of my life.

The second dream came a few years after I had been born again. I had become concerned about my place in Christ. I wanted much more assurance as to the reality of growing in Jesus. I fell asleep with this thought on my mind. As I slept, the following dream occurred, so vivid it is still crystal clear in my memory. I was standing on a precipice looking through a telescopic camera at acres and acres of vineyards. The camera zoomed in on a particular vineyard and slowly zoomed to one particular vine. The camera panned up the vine to a healthy branch. I knew intuitively that branch was me. I was so happy I can remember the encouragement I felt.

As I thanked the Lord, the camera began to slowly pan out from the vine. The vine showed healthy growth and many beautiful leaves. After the camera had panned out about 25 feet, there at the end of the branch was one rather puny grape. Then the camera stopped. As I looked at the grape I heard a voice say, "Son, look at all the branches and leaves that have gone into producing that one grape." I looked and sure enough there were about 25 feet of branches and leaves. Then I heard the voice say, "Son, all of that to produce one grape, do you want me to do it?"

I knew instantly the voice was asking for permission to prune the branch, but would not do it without my permission. I shuddered and weakly said, "Go ahead but please do it quickly!" The point being made was that although the life in the branch was not evil but good, it wasn't producing much fruit. Most of the life was going to produce branch and leaf. I also knew intuitively I could spend the rest of my life producing leaves and branches. The voice also communicated that He would never condemn me if I chose that life. The voice desired for me to freely choose to receive the pruning and produce grapes. The issue was never good and evil but fruitfulness. I chose fruitfulness as I had learned that the best grapes come from vines that have been under the pruner's knife the longest. I closed my eyes and said, "Do it." Then I woke up.

The third dream came after several years in denominational ministry in Tulsa. I had been concerned about how Christ in the church was to approach the world. I fell asleep thinking long and hard on the subject. Again the Lord visited me in my sleep. In the dream I was suspended above downtown Tulsa. As I looked over the city, a giant hand broke through the clouds and picked up a large church. The hand plucked it up as though it were an onion or carrot and disappeared back through the clouds.

A short time later as I pondered the scene, the hand broke through the clouds again, this time holding the church upside down. The hand was shaking the church and a white substance came out of its bell tower and covered the city. The hand shook the church with greater and greater urgency until it disappeared once again back up through the clouds. I thought to myself that obviously the church was to have been a dispenser of salt.

I had just about come to this conclusion when the hand again broke through the clouds. This time, though, the hand furiously threw the church down with great force where it splattered all over the city. The hand disappeared back through the clouds. I waited for what seemed like a long time, but the hand never returned. As I waited, I pondered the previous actions of the hand, the church, the white stuff, and the fury with which the church had been thrown down. I descended to the street level and, wetting my finger, tasted the white stuff. Immediately I spit it out. It was talcum powder. I woke up! I read Matthew 5:13 where the Lord tells us that we are to be the salt of the world. May we ever be so!

9. What Does Healthy Discipleship Look Like?

As a Christian minister with some 50 years worth of experience working with God's people and as someone who was a mid-level leader in the Shepherding Movement in the 1980's, I have strong opinions in the area of discipleship. This has always been a strong desire of my heart: to produce healthy and committed disciples for Jesus.

To put it as simply as I can, discipleship is authored by Jesus and the Holy Spirit as believers participate in resurrection life together. Discipleship is not hierarchical, or based on human authority, in the sense of one person legalistically submitting to another. That, sadly, is primarily how we practiced it in the Shepherding Movement. Rather, true discipleship works itself out as believers follow the leading of the Holy Spirit as they experience life together.

Here are two examples of discipleship that I experienced. One turned out to be life giving; the other turned out the opposite. In the shepherding movement, the process involved putting more mature believers in positions of authority over less mature believers. This was what we called "lesser to greater." But what happened was that this hierarchical relationship ending up drawing people away from a personal relationship with Jesus. Rather than Jesus leading His sheep, the process made the younger believers dependent on the person placed above them. The process eventually worked in such a way that the "greater" would fix "the lesser."

While it was true that some real Holy Spirit discipleship took place in the midst of the movement, on the whole, the damage this caused was great. The reason for this was that the disciplers, the persons in the position of authority, tended to grow ever more suspicious of the ability of those under them to hear the voice of God for themselves. The result was that the younger believers would develop an ongoing and unhealthy dependence on the established authority structure. This effectively replaced Jesus as their Shepherd and negated His promise of personal relationship with each of those who follow Him.

On the positive side of discipleship were the experiences that Barbara and I had with young men and women who would come to us on their own initiative and ask if they could live with us and our five children. Our response surprised even us as we gladly and joyfully said, "Yes!" Most of them stayed for a couple of years while they continued to work and live life with us. Many others came for shorter periods of time and we blessed them on their way in Jesus. There were no classes or curriculum; it was just "life together." The joy these young men and women brought to our family and to the Lord continues to this day decades later. Watching their lives over the decades as they have married, raised families and gone on into the calling of God for their lives humbles and blesses Barbara and me immensely.

The discipleship took place as the Holy Spirit enabled them and Barbara and me to love Jesus and live our lives to His glory. Years later these same men and women would do the same with their families and other younger men and women. No structure; just life together on a daily basis. This kind of life cannot be managed or structured; it can only be lived.

Here is the wisdom of God that Barbara and I have gained

over the years and still continue to learn. When Jesus said that he would make fishers of men, he didn't mean "catch and control." I believe the disciples could leave any time they wished. They stayed because as Peter said in John 6:68, after Jesus asked them if they wanted to go away; "Lord to whom shall we go? You have the words of eternal life. And we have believed that you are the Holy One of God." They stayed with Jesus because of the Holy Spirit's call and sustaining love and power. They didn't stay because Jesus had a program they committed themselves to but a relationship of love drawn by the Holy Spirit.

This was authenticated by Jesus in Matthew 16:13-20 where Jesus told his followers that only by revelation would he build his church. To put it in my words, you cannot have discipleship without revelation as the foundational and sustaining power. What kind of revelation? In Matthew 16: 13-20, the Lord says that only the Holy Spirit can reveal who Jesus is and therefore the church must be built upon that revelation alone. That revelation of who He is must be given personally to every member in the church. Then we will have a solid foundation on which to be built together. No membership role, or title, or command can author true discipleship. I am not implying that Barbara and I were and continue to be Jesus. But I will say that we represented him by his grace to many men

and women both single and married. We desired only to "bless and release" them into their God given callings. Our intention was never to keep or control them but to love, bless and release.

An example of that is a young man named Kenny. About a decade ago Kenny and his wife joined our fellowship. As time passed they were trying to figure out what their future was supposed to look like.

As we talked with them over the course of a year and a half
Kenny became clear that the Lord was honoring his heart's
desire to be an artist. The problem was how to support his
family. After taking on many odd jobs, the continuing longing
to express his artistic call would not go away. Eventually
they decided to move to an art community in New Mexico to
facilitate the desire of their hearts. We were sad to see them
go as there was such a sweet gentle heart in both of them, and
their presence in our fellowship was very encouraging. We bid
them goodbye with prayer and blessing. On the eve of their
leaving, Kenny brought a gift to our home. He said the gift
was the best way for him to express his thanks for our love and
fellowship. That gift was the charcoal rendering of me on this
page. I was and am still deeply moved by the sketch. I think of
it as one of the sweet gifts from God I have received over the
years. If we as a fellowship had tried to "capture" Kenny and
encourage him to stay in our group, rather than allowing him to
follow of the Lord's Spirit within, we would have done him a
disservice.

In John chapters 13-17, Jesus prepared the disciples to
reproduce by the same means He did: by the Life of the Holy
Spirit within them. In Luke 24 we read the story of Jesus on
the road to Emmaus with two of his disciples. Their eyes were
prevented from recognizing Him, and only as He broke the
bread later and disappeared did they understand. As they said
in verse 32, "Were not our hearts burning within us while He
was speaking to us on the road, while He was explaining the
Scriptures to us? " That burning within them was what I have
been referring to in this book as "the voice in the belly," that is,
the Holy Spirit that Jesus promised to send to live in us forever.
All of Christian living, including discipleship, was to flow out
of that life force within.

To again paraphrase a metaphor: Jesus did not catch men
to bind them to religious activity or institutions but so they
would freely be bound to Him forever. That is the desire of the
Lord when He calls us into relationships where discipleship

takes place. We don't control or manipulate; we love and teach through our lives. That is the best kind of discipleship.

10. Four Experiences God Uses to Change Lives

While there are many experiences the Lord takes us through to draw us to Himself, there are four in particular that have been present in my life. Though they might surprise you, they are Success, Failure, Heresy, and Betrayal.

The first two go together easily as they arise out of the Tree of the Knowledge of Good and Evil. While success might seem to be good and failure might seem to be bad or evil, as a motivation they both stem from the wrong source. I contend that the presence of either in a believer's life does not necessarily show the presence or absence of God's blessing. The fruit of success is often arrogance, becoming judgmental, and at times, the practice of fleshly religion. How many so called successful people can you think of who are prideful, look down on others and consider their way of practicing faith superior to all others though it may cause deep division. On the other hand, how many people do you know who have gone through failure and loss who have come out on the other side humble, kind, and sensitive to the Lord's leading in themselves and others.

Undue attention to success or failure manifests itself in what I call the "tyranny of self." When I live my life according to my measure of whether I am outwardly succeeding or failing, my Christian life naturally becomes all about me and how I'm doing. Over the years I personally tried hard to be a "good" Christian. I experienced some success in Christian self-promotion in my efforts to serve God. I became well known in some circles and with the right moves could easily have had my name up in lights. Nevertheless there was always uneasiness in me that something was wrong whether I received the applause of my contemporaries or their criticism.

This way of living produced in me a roller-coaster life devoid of any true and lasting fruit. Oh, success may look and sound good, but let me assure you that living for success only exalts the flesh. That is not God's highest and best way for us. He desires for us to live out of the Tree of Life, a picture of the Lord Jesus. Jesus alone can give success and true fruitfulness, along with the loving godly disciplines that enable us to focus on Him and not default to our "old man" or the flesh and its seductive ways. The difference is life and death. I pray that others who face the same tyranny of living by the wrong tree may learn from my experience and turn to Jesus in a new way. Don't measure your life by what you consider to be success or failure. That's a dead end street. Trust Jesus that as you look to Him, he will become your desire and you will walk in the good deeds that he has prepared for you.

The third experience the Lord used in my life arose out of my desire to help him out in the area of theology. That experience is being part of a good heresy. What I mean by that is believing with all your heart a theology you're convinced is God's leading and then finding out you were completely wrong. I don't mean a little wrong, I mean totally wrong. For me the heresy involved giving myself fully to the Shepherding Movement as I speak of earlier in the book.

I am not laying blame here at the feet of the godly men who desired nothing more than seeing people grow in Christ. The fault, and the core of the heresy, lay in the belief that we who were the "shepherds" were to fix people under our care by our covering protection and wisdom, as they submitted to our authority. The fruit was mixed at best and hellish at worst. I thank God for His gift of repentance that freed me from a life of regret and the opportunities to go to those I had directly led astray or wounded in some manner. Let me state with clarity that this particular heresy is not the only one as there are many out there in the religious world wounding the sheep of God even as I write. Thankfully, God is bigger than all of them and He can graciously show us the missteps we make as we seek to follow Him. He guides and corrects, leading us into an ever growing revelation of how great He is. Have you bought full scale into a belief system about God that turned out to be off the mark? Don't despair. You are not alone.

Lastly there is betrayal. By that I mean having the sense (more than the sense, actually the experience) of being turned on by a trusted friend or cared for brother or sister in the body of Christ and watching them try to deeply hurt or destroy you. I remember going through this experience only too well. Most people who try and provide leadership roles in the functioning of the body of Christ will know such pain. Of course the counter is true as well. Sadly, many who lead in the body use the tactic of betrayal to weaken and harm those they are threatened by. In most cases it's likely that our betrayers feel fully justified in their actions, often even carrying them out in the Lord's Name. That only makes it hurt all the more.

How do we as believers wanting to stay soft before the Lord Jesus endure such experiences without becoming bitter and vindictive ourselves? Our dear Lord Jesus helped me as no other could by leading me painfully through the forgiveness I needed to truly experience not just in word but reality. That forgiveness for my betrayers finally came after several months with at least two revelations. One is that only Jesus could enable me to forgive, and secondly, discovering that I had the capacity to betray others myself. Once I got in touch with those two realities it has helped me to keep my heart tender daily before the Lord and His people. As I think about those who practice such behavior now, I realize, truly, "there, but for the grace of God go I."

Have you gone through such an experience? I hope that if you are still suffering under the pain, the Lord will lead you into His forgiveness, soften your heart, and enable you to walk forward in His gracious presence. Again, you are not alone and your Jesus is big enough to "restore the years the locusts have eaten" as the prophet Joel said.

As said earlier, no doubt there are many experiences that the Lord uses to mold and make us into His image. My hope is that should any of these four have come your way, or await you in the future, you can know that the Lord is great enough to use them to his advantage to enable you to love and follow him more closely.

Here are links to websites that contain more of Tom and Barbara's teaching ministry:

http://thenobleheart.com/media/podcasts/

Talking with a Sage, an interview with Gary Barkalow and Jeff Andrechyn

http://www.lifestream.org/god-journey/keeper-and-kept

An interview with Wayne Jacobsen

www.mohnministriesbookstore.com

AFTERWORD

As I look back upon our story, I am again struck with the goodness and patience of our Lord Jesus. Eternally speaking our journey on Earth is very short but it is more than enough time to long for the Kingdom to come on Earth as it is "already" in heaven. Barbara and I have truly tasted of that Kingdom now and we know to participate in the Kingdom to come will be a privilege beyond words. My prayer is that our journey will encourage you the reader in experiencing now, the Kingdom present. I believe that every true believer lives in the tension of the Kingdom now and the Kingdom to come. The Kingdom now is more than enough to enable us to "finish the race" with perseverance and joy unspeakable and full of glory.

The recollections contained in this book are but a small sample of our Lord's mighty hand throughout our lives. I end with the words of John as he ended his gospel, *"And there are also many other things which Jesus did, which if they were written in detail. I suppose that even the world itself would not contain the books which were written."* John 21:25.

With gratitude beyond words, your brethren, Tom and Barbara Mohn, truly "Pilgrims."

PICTURE CREDITS

Page 6: Tom and Barbara Mohn, 2012

Page 12: File Photo, Dr. Martin Luther King marching with supporters, Selma, Alabama, March, 1965

Page 31: Tom in the Wesley Boys Choir; photo circa 1944

Page 35: Young Tom at home, 1944

Page 37: Tom at home, 1945

Page 42: Senior Prom Photo; Tom went with Bobbi the girl who was his first love and helped him through his healing from the auto accident. 1953

Page 44: ROTC photo prior to entering the Army: 1953

Page 48: Barbara, Rebecca, and Tom at Kendall College, 1963

Page 68: Baptism in Tulsa by lifelong friend Rev Bill Sanders 1967

Page 83: Tom Mohn 1965

Page 116: Newspaper File Photo showing Rev. Charlie Groves in North Tulsa. He served as Associate Pastor at Centenary United Methodist church; 1968

Page 117 : Newspaper File Photo: Spring 1968 before leaving for Virginia

Page 126: Home meetings that became Bread of Life Fellowship had begun in 1968. This photo was taken just before leaving Oral Roberts University, 1971.

Page 133: On the air with "Good Morning Brother Pilgrim." Photo taken at KORU radio station at Oral Roberts University. Tom was radio announcer and General Manager of KORU. from 1968-1971

Page 161: Tom and Barbara after leaving the Shepherding Movement in 1979

Page 166: Tom and Barbara after retiring from Bread of Life in 2003 and continuing ministry through "Mohn Ministries". Picture circa 2011

Page 195: Kenny's charcoal sketch of Tom

Page 203: Top photo: Tom and Barbara with their five children and their spouses: Easter 2013

Page 203: Bottom photo: Tom and Barb at home with 19 out of their 21 grandchildren: Easter 2013